FRANCIS,
BISHOP OF ROME

Michael Collins

Francis, Bishop of Rome

A SHORT BIOGRAPHY

MISERANDO ATQUE ELIGENDO

the columba press

Published in 2013 by

the columba press

55A Spruce Avenue,
Stillorgan Industrial Park,
Blackrock, Co. Dublin

Cover by Patrick O'Donoghue
Cover image courtesy of L'Osservatore Romano
Origination by The Columba Press
Printed in Ireland by SPRINT-print Ltd

ISBN 9781 78218 066 1

TABLE OF CONTENTS

Early Life

In September 1929 the twenty-one-year-old Mario José Bergoglio, father of the future pope, embarked on a ship in the Italian port of Genoa. The vessel, the *Giulio Caesare*, was bound for South America. For the young man, the journey offered the exciting prospect of starting a new life and perhaps a family in the New World.

With his father and mother, Giovanni and Rosa, the young man had travelled to Argentina slightly later than planned. Originally the family had intended to sail some years earlier on the *Principessa Mafalda*. The vessel's voyage ended in disaster when the ocean liner was shipwrecked off the coast of Brazil, a tragedy in which hundreds of passengers were drowned. The Bergoglio's delay in travelling had doubtlessly saved their lives.

Argentina had become a welcoming haven for thousands of European emigrants who made their home in the southern climes. Article 25 of the 1853 Constitution stated that:

> *The Federal Government will encourage European immigration, and it will not restrict, limit or burden with any taxes the entrance into Argentine territory of foreigners who come with the goal of working the land, improving the industries and teaching the sciences and the arts.*

Between 1914 to 1947, the population of Argentina rose from 7.9 million to 15.8 million. The two largest blocks of settlers came from Spain and Italy. By 1947, 1.4 million Italians had settled in Argentina in the hope of finding prosperity and civil stability. That number had increased dramatically during and following the Second World War.

The attractive prospect offered by Argentina was all the more appealing to the Bergoglio family. For years they had watched the rise of Fascism in Italy. The fascist party, the Blackshirts, were founded in 1919 by a right-wing soldier, Benito Mussolini. By mid-1922, the party had amassed considerable political support and was about to seize power in Italy. The Bergoglio's did not support the party or its divisive politics. Along with many other Italians, the Bergoglio family believed that only by leaving their homeland could they save their traditions and values.

The Bergoglio's had left Portacomaro, a small town in the province of Asti, some 48 kilometres from Turin. For generations the family had lived at Bricco Marmorito, a few kilometres from Asti. The portal of the door of the ancestral home still bears a ceramic tile which reads *Signore, benedici chi entra in questa casa* (Lord, bless whomsoever enters this house).

The homestead, along with land and a small vineyard, was bought by four Bergoglio brothers in 1854 from a Jewish vendor. Over the years the family had expanded. Some worked the land while others were engaged in commerce in the town.

In the early 20th century, the family established a small confectioner's shop. When various members of the family decided to emigrate, the decision was taken to sell the shop and house and join their relatives in their new homeland.

On 15 February 1930, the ship, the *Giulio Caesare* landed in Buenos Aires, at the end of a six-month voyage. After some calls at the ports of Europe, the ship had undertaken the long journey to the Americas. Despite the warm weather in Buenos Aires, Rosa Bergoglio wore a coat with a fur collar. Inside the lining of the collar were stitched Italian lire, the result of the sale of their property, which she had smuggled out of Italy. Passing unnoticed through the Customs office, the family descended the gangway onto the large square in front of the dockyard. The money in Rosa's collar would be enough to make a new start in Argentina.

South America would be their homeland for the rest of their lives. Work was plentiful, civil strife was rare and social prospects were good. Moreover, three grand-uncles of the future pope had emigrated to Parana in 1922, where they had set up a small paving company. The area was thriving and construction opportunities were plentiful.

Unlike most migrants arriving in Buenos Aires, the Bergoglio's did not need to stay in the hostel for migrants or register for work. With family connections, they could settle immediately into their new surroundings.

Welcomed at the dock by their relatives, the Bergoglio's were escorted to the family home at Flores. This was a district close to the city centre, favoured by Italian migrants. The Italian population was so dense that most elderly Italians spoke their native dialect rather than learn Spanish.

With the arrival of Giovanni, four of the brothers now lived in Argentina; one brother and a sister remained in Italy. The Bergoglio family in Buenos Aires was expanding. The brothers had built a house on four floors thanks to the success of their construction enterprise. Each brother occupied a floor, leaving the ground level to be shared in common by family members, visitors and neighbours. The floors were reached by an elevator, the first to be built in the city of Buenos Aires. There was also a small cupola on the roof. The new arrivals settled in well. The climate was agreeable and the people welcoming.

Within three years of the Bergoglio family's arrival, however, Argentina experienced a dramatic financial crisis. In 1932 the building trade collapsed, and the Bergoglio's were obliged to sell the house in which they lived. Even the family tomb had to be sold. One of the three brothers, the head of the paving firm, had died from cancer and another brother borrowed 2,000 pesos in order to buy a store and some stock. Mario had trained in Italy as an accountant and although his degree was not recognised in Argentina, he helped in the running of the new business with his accountancy skills. Through hard work and determination, the brothers managed to survive the crisis, although they were unable to revive the family fortunes entirely. Nonetheless, they had work, and once more were stable.

In 1934, Mario met a young Argentinian woman, Regina María Sivori. Her mother was of Genoese and Piedmont origin, while her father was Argentinian, descended from Genoese stock. The couple met at a social function in the parish of San Antonio in Almagro. The following year, on 12 December 1935, they were married in the local church.

The newly-weds bought a house in the district of Flores to remain close to their families; number 500 calle Membrillar, close to Plaza de la Misericordia. The house was small, with a large kitchen and hearth. In this home the couple's five children were to be reared.

On 17 December 1936, Regina María gave birth to her firstborn. He was called Jorge, a name frequently used within the family. It was the fourth centenary since the foundation of Buenos Aires. A week later, on Christmas Day, the infant was baptised in the Basilica of San Carlos Borromeo by the Salesian priest, Father Enrique Pozzoli. This priest was to have a great influence on young Jorge and he later became the youth's spiritual director. The infant's godparents were Francisco Sivori and Rosa Vassallo de Bergoglio.

The church, a magnificent neo-Gothic building, was to play an important role in the development of the young man. Here he served Mass and took part in the many annual feast days and processions popular among the Italian community. The great songwriter, actor and proponent of the tango, Carlos Gardel sang in the choir as a youth. Another notable past-member of the parish choir was the native Indian of Patagonia, Blessed Ceferino Namuncurá, a Salesian seminarian who died in 1905. The parish contained a large number of migrants from Turin, a city important in the life of St John Bosco, founder of the Salesian Order.

Throughout Jorge's childhood the Bergoglio family attended the annual feast day procession in honour of Our Lady Help of Christians on 24 May. An image of Our Lady hung in the kitchen of the family home. Jorge retained his special devotion to Mary the Mother of Jesus, as well as a particular devotion to St Joseph. The devotional life of the Italian community in Buenos Aires, their attachment to the saints and their parish, was fundamental to the spiritual make up of the young Jorge.

Jorge recalls with great affection his grandmother Rosa. When he was just 13 months old, his mother gave birth to a second son, Alberto Horacio. With a second infant in the house, Regina María needed help. The family could not afford assistance and the grandmother was eager to help. Each day Rosa came to collect her grandson and brought the infant to her house. There she fed and cared for him until the evening, when he was returned to his parents. It was as a very young child that he learned Italian at his grandmother's knee. His grandparents and his uncles spoke the Piedmontese dialect between themselves. It was the language of a far away land which belonged in the past. He noted the tinge of nostalgia in their voices as they spoke of people that he had never heard of and whom they never would see again.

Jorge's father never spoke to him in Italian, anxious that his son would be fluent rather in Spanish. Years later, Jorge would have reason to appreciate the Italian he had learned from his older relatives. His father had little interest in maintaining the old language or traditions. He was firmly focused on the future and immersed himself in his new culture. Although Mario spoke Spanish with a lilting Italian accent, he regarded himself as Argentinian. He always spoke Castilian Spanish with his children. Bedtime stories, however, were usually tales from Italy. At Christmas, the family celebrated the arrival of the fabled La Befana, the good witch who visits children on 6 January.

As a child, Jorge was enrolled in the nearby San Juan Bosco school on Calle Varela. Throughout his life he retained a special affection for the Salesian nuns who taught him. As a priest and later bishop, he always returned once a year to celebrate Mass for the community.

The family was extremely united and spent a great deal of time together. Every Sunday the family attended Mass together in the local parish church of San José. Then while Mario took the children for a walk, Regina María returned to finish preparing lunch.

Days after his election, María Elena spoke to Italian journalists and recounted some details of her childhood. The entire family, which sometimes numbered more than twenty, dined in the kitchen. Among the dishes remembered years later by María Elena were cappelletti, home-made pasta with ragù, Piedmontese risotto, roast chicken and vegetables. As in many Italian families of the time, the table was the most important piece of furniture in the house. Here food was served and the table became a focal point.

On Sundays there were six or seven courses. The main dish was usually roast chicken and the meal concluded with a desert. Grandmother Rosa taught María to cook. When she married Mario, María often joked, she did not even know how to fry an egg!

Rosa had an enormous influence on her grandchildren. She told them stories about her homeland, and recounted how once she had mounted a pulpit in the local church to denounce Mussolini. She told them fables and tales from Italy, a land which seemed quite magical to them. Speaking decades later to Fr Juan Isasmendi on the parish radio of Villa 21, Jorge recalled 'The one who had the greatest impact on me was my grandmother, who taught me the faith and read me the lives of the saints.' Many years later, as his grandmother was dying in a nursing home run by the Camillan Sisters, Jorge faithfully visited her most days. 'This is the most important moment of her life,' he told one of the sisters as he held his grandmother's hand. 'She is going before the Lord.'

All the children were deeply attached to their parents. Jorge recalls his father's cheerfulness and his optimism. He never saw him angry although María Elena recalled that he was able to discipline the children with a single glance. The children knew that authority lay with the father but that they could always get their mother to intervene. The couple were deeply in love and Mario regularly brought his wife flowers and small tokens.

When he returned home in the evening, Mario would put his heavy ledgers on the table and turn on the gramophone. The house, according to María Elena, was always full of music. Opera was the favourite choice, followed by the tango. The children all learned to dance at home. After dinner, Mario visited his uncles and neighbours, where the conversation was always in Italian.

At weekends, Jorge attended football matches played by the local club, San Lorenzo de Almagro. The club, founded in 1908 at the nearby chapel of Saint Anthony by the Salesian priest, Fr Lorenzo Massa, was at the centre of the sporting life of the district. The priest founded the club when a young boy was killed by a passing tram while playing on the street. Mario played basketball in the club and was a loyal supporter, although Jorge alone of the children, shared his father's passion. Jorge also learned to play basketball and football. He was to remain a lifelong fan of San Lorenzo, with its red and blue strip.

Mario and Regina María had five children, Jorge, Alberto Horacio, Oscar Adrian, Marta Regina and María Elena. Before the birth of her last born, Regina María suffered a miscarriage. With the birth of her fifth child, Regina María was temporarily paralysed. The children were required to help around the house and do all the chores necessary. Jorge learned to cook during this time. His mother measured out the ingredients while he boiled the water and prepared the food.

Among his fondest memories was sitting in the afternoons with his mother and siblings, listening to opera on the radio. As a famous aria was about to begin, Regina María would say 'Listen, this is going to be a beautiful song.' While the music wafted through the house, María darned and mended clothes. It was from their mother that the five children learned frugality. If a piece of material was worn out in one shape, it was recycled to make something serviceable.

When the young Jorge was 13 and had finished primary school, his father told him that he was old enough to find a job. Although the family was relatively well off, his father explained the importance of work, at least in the summer months. While the family did not possess a car or take summer vacations, they were comfortable. Mario had found employment as an accountant. Jorge was surprised at his father's insistence that he find a part-time job but he did not protest and his father taught him the rudiments of accountancy.

Some weeks later, with the help of a family friend, Jorge got a job cleaning at the Hickthier–Bachmann hosiery factory. Here he worked each morning from 7.00 a.m. until 1.00 p.m. After two years, at the age of 15, he entered the administration area. While maintaining the part-time job, Jorge continued with his studies at the then Industrial No. 12. In the fourth year he began to pursue a course in chemistry at an industrial college, *Escuela Nacional de Educación Técnica,* dividing his time between study and work. While he continued to work each morning until one in the afternoon, he was obliged to attend lectures until 8.00 p.m.

In retrospect, Jorge was grateful to his father for his insistence that he both work and study. In later life, he met a great number of unemployed people. He realised that work is not simply an obligation but also a human right. When it is taken away, people lose the creative part of their personality and existence. The work experience taught him also to value money and to avoid waste and excess.

During these years he became an avid reader, in particular Dante, Manzoni and Hölderlin. His work supervisor at the factory, Esther Balarino de Careaga from Paraguay, was an ardent Communist and encouraged Jorge in his pursuit of knowledge. The young man was greatly influenced by Esther's passion for politics which he grew to share. He read Communist literature which Esther gave him. The Church was strictly opposed to atheistic Communism, and thus Jorge did not embrace the ideology. Some years later Jorge learned that Esther's daughter and son-in-law were abducted and she herself was kidnapped along with two nuns during the civil disturbances of the 1970s. She died in captivity, having been tortured. She remains one of the most influential people in young Jorge's life.

From Esther, Jorge realised that work is fundamental and lies at the centre of the social fabric. When he graduated from college with a diploma, the young man intended to become a professional chemical engineer. But even then he felt his life was changing.

Jorge was interested in social work and joined the local branch of Catholic Action, a social outreach programme for young Catholics. He spent time with his friends during his free time and learned the tango dance. Although a shy youth, he mixed easily within his circle of friends. These were also years marked by political unrest in Argentina.

When he was seventeen, Jorge had an intense spiritual experience. On 21 September 1953, the first day of Argentinian spring, Jorge and a group of companions had decided to go for a picnic. The day is an important day for young people. Jorge later confided to his sister that he had intended to propose to a girl that same day, to be engaged.

On his way to the gathering, Jorge went to Confession at the church of San Jose de Flores. Speaking with Fr Duarte, whom he had never met before, the young man changed his mind and decided to first try his vocation to the priesthood. For Jorge, the encounter would always be seen as providential. He recounted the day half a century later.

> During that Confession, something strange happened to me. I cannot say what it was, but it was something that changed my life. I could say that it was as if I had been caught off guard ... From that moment onwards, God became for me the one who goes ahead. You do not seek him, He seeks you first.

Although he thought about becoming a priest he was undecided on what order or diocese he should enter. He continued to study more and pray about a possible vocation. Four years were to pass before he finally made up his mind to try his religious vocation.

When he was 21, Jorge nearly lost his life. For several days he had felt unwell, with a rising temperature. His mother called a doctor to visit him at home. The doctor advised that he be admitted to hospital. Each day the doctors administered drugs and tried to discover the cause of an infection which caused him shortness of breath. He grasped his mother's arm.

'Tell me, what is happening?'

Finally the diagnosis was made. He was suffering with a severe form of pneumonia. Three cysts had appeared on the upper part of his lung. Not responding to conventional medication, the decision was made to operate. The right lung was severely affected and the surgeon removed the upper part of the organ. For three days the young man hung between life and death. Each day the lungs were drained and fresh bandages applied. The procedure to drain the lungs caused immense distress and pain.

One day, Jorge received a visit from Sr Dolores, the nun who had prepared him for his First Communion. She was deeply upset to see him in agony and explained to him that he was suffering like Jesus on the cross. These words proved an unexpected help to the young man on the verge of his maturity. While others simply wished him a speedy recovery, her words made sense.

Jorge continued his recuperation, even undertaking a journey to the plains of Tandil. His parents were relieved with their son's progress and went on a pilgrimage of thanksgiving to the shrine of Our Lady of Luján. They also presumed that he would continue with further studies in chemistry which would advance his career. When he returned home, Regina María cleared out a small area in the upper story of the house, overlooking a small terrace. Here Jorge would be able to study in peace. As the eldest, Jorge was looked up to by his siblings. They were told to be quiet while he was studying and sent to play outside.

One day, while dusting the area, Jorge's mother looked at the books her son was studying. She was surprised to find several books of theology. She had to wait until evening when he returned home to confront him on his choice of reading material. When he returned that evening, she asked why he had lied to her.

'I did not lie, Mama,' replied Jorge. 'I am studying medicine, but medicine of the soul.'

To his surprise, Regina María reacted badly to the news of her son's vocation, realising that soon he would leave home to study at a seminary. She continuously pleaded with him to delay his decision. He was, she insisted, still young and immature. Jorge's father was pleased with the news, as was his grandmother Rosa. According to María Elena, 'Papa would have been pleased if we all had become nuns and priests!'

Jorge decided that he would like to be a diocesan priest and work in Buenos Aires. He entered the archdiocesan seminary Immaculada Concepción in Villa Devoto. Here he spent three happy years, but he was not sure if he had discerned his vocation correctly. He loved his native city, but he felt drawn to spread the faith beyond his country as a missionary. He also considered becoming a Salesian priest, as he wanted to work with young people.

Inspired by Jesuit priests who assisted at the diocesan seminary, Jorge approached the vocations director for the order. After a period of reflection and with the permission of the rector, Jorge decided to join the Jesuit Order. As he explained in later years, he was particularly attracted to the sense of order and discipline evident in the Jesuit way of life. He had now changed his mind with regard to his native diocese. The idea of serving on the missions appealed to him as he gained confidence. In particular, he wished to go to Japan, where the Jesuits had long since had an important presence.

On 11 March 1958 Jorge entered the Society of Jesus. After a brief preparation in Córdoba, Jorge travelled to Santiago, Chile where he entered the novitiate. The following year he was to experience the first great bereavement of his life when his father died of a sudden heart attack. The death of the head of the family caused Jorge immense grief. He considered returning to his mother to help her bring up his siblings. In the end, he decided to remain in college and dedicate himself to his studies.

His mother made one visit to her son in Chile, although she confided in him that it was not easy and had taken a long time to decide upon.

THE SOCIETY OF JESUS

The Society of Jesus, popularly called the Jesuits, was founded in 1540 by the Spaniard Ignatius of Loyola. For almost half a millennium, it has been one of the most important and influential religious orders in the Catholic Church.

Ignatius was born on 23 October 1491 at Azpeitia, a town in the northern Basque region of Spain. The family came from minor nobility. The youngest of 13 children, Ignatius' mother died soon after his birth. He was then brought up by the daughter of the local blacksmith. At the age of 17, having trained as a page at the court of a relative, Juan Velázquez de Cuéllar, Ignatius entered the service of Antonio Manrique de Lara, the Duke of Nájera and the Viceroy of Navarre. A military career awaited him.

The young man became a successful soldier and participated in a number of battles until he was seriously wounded during the Siege of Pamplona in May 1521. A cannonball shattered his leg and left him crippled. He was operated on to repair the wound.

During his long recuperation, Ignatius read a number of spiritual texts. On his recovery he made a votive pilgrimage of thanksgiving to the sanctuary of Our Lady of Montserrat near Barcelona. Here, on 25 March 1522, he left his sword and dagger as he embraced a new way of life. Rejecting his luxurious clothing and his military decorations, he adopted a simple black gown. He spent the next 10 months in Manresa living in a cave and it was here that he began to formulate the Spiritual Exercises, one of the most famous spiritual treatises in 16th-century Europe. The following year, Ignatius travelled to the Holy Land to satiate his curiosity about the places where Jesus had lived.

After his return to Spain, Ignatius decided to devote himself entirely to the promotion and defence of the Catholic faith, sometimes preaching in the marketplace. He also studied at the Universities of Alcalá and Salamanca before enrolling at the University of Paris in the summer of 1528 to study theology.

During seven formative years in Paris, Ignatius made several friends among the student body. Six of these became close companions. Four were Spanish and the band was completed by a Portuguese and French companion.

The Church was engaged in a crisis caused by the criticisms of a number of reformers. Luther, Calvin, Zwingli and other zealous Christians proposed dramatic action to excise corruption and hypocrisy in the Catholic Church.

The papacy was slow in reacting efficiently to the proposals of the reformers. Rather than accept the many valid criticisms, the pontiffs rejected their efforts and condemned their teachings. The tardy response not only delayed Church reform but also led to decades of civil wars throughout Europe.

The six companions discussed ways of assisting their fellow Catholics and refuting heresy. On 15 August 1534, Ignatius and his companions attended Mass at the Church of Our Lady of the Martyrs at Montmartre in Paris. In the crypt of the Church they took vows of poverty and chastity, offering their lives for the defence of the Catholic faith.

In the succeeding years, Ignatius suffered poor health. With his companions, he petitioned the pope for an audience. The companions wanted papal direction to set up a religious order, which would ensure young members for the future.

Although he had been ordained in June 1537, Ignatius waited for more than a year before celebrating Mass. On Christmas Day, 1538, Ignatius celebrated his first Mass in the Basilica of St Mary Major's in Rome. According to a pious legend, the manger in which Jesus was believed to have been born had been brought to Rome centuries earlier.

In 1540, the society received papal recognition and two years later Ignatius was elected General of the newly-founded order. In addition to the traditional vows of poverty, chastity and obedience, Ignatius and his followers took a fourth vow of fidelity to the Pope. This fourth vow required the companions to put themselves at the disposal of the Roman pontiff and carry out any missions he may charge them with, particularly to the education of the youth and missionary work.

Although the Society was properly known as the Society of Jesus, the term Jesuit was first used in 1544, in a derogatory manner. The term was never used by Ignatius himself as it mocked somebody who employed the name of Jesus excessively in conversation. Gradually, however, the term was appropriated by the members and came to be used in a positive sense.

During the following decade, the Society of Jesus experienced rapid growth. The Jesuits were decisive in launching the Catholic Reformation, a response to the fracturing of the Christian faith in Europe. Many reformers had attacked the corruption in the papacy and the clergy in general. Within a few years, hundreds had joined the Company of Jesus. By Ignatius' death in Rome in 1556 the members of the Society were engaged in missions in Europe, India, China and Japan. With particular dedication to the education of young people, the Jesuits set up schools and universities, raising the standard of education.

Ignatius' sanctity impressed a wide circle. The service offered by the Jesuits was recognised by successive popes. On 12 March 1622, Ignatius was canonised by Pope Gregory XV. For more than a century the Jesuits flourished, establishing educational academies and expanding missions in various lands. Towards the end of the 18th century, disaster struck the order.

In 1773, Pope Clement XIV issued a decree suppressing the Society of Jesus. The Jesuits had become numerous and powerful but had also gained many enemies who viewed them with suspicion and mistrust. Clement acceded to political pressure from several European countries, some of which desired to seize Jesuit assets.

While the order managed to survive in some countries such as Prussia, the widespread abolition was reversed by Pope Pius VII in 1814. In the period following the restoration, the influence of the Jesuits expanded once more. By the middle of the 20th century, the order had reached its numerical zenith.

During the post-Vatican II period and especially under the pontificate of John Paul II, the Jesuits experienced tensions between the order and the papacy. Other religious organisations such as Opus Dei, Communion and Liber-ation and the Legionaries of Christ gained the pontiff's esteem.

The General of the Jesuits, Pedro Arrupe (1965–83) refocused the order, emphasising the members' care for the poor. This 'option for the poor,' was most notable in the work of the South American Jesuits. In some places their work provoked violent opposition. On 16 November 1989 six Jesuits, along with a housekeeper and her daughter, were murdered on the campus of the Central American University in El Salvador by the military.

Today the Jesuits form the largest single religious order in the Catholic Church, numbering over 17,000 members, dispersed throughout 119 countries on six continents. Their work has diversified to schools and universities, hospitals and scientific research, culture and communications, as well as philosophy and theology. Ignatius' initial vision for his clerics was one of military discipline. Part of the charism is the successful manner in which members are enabled to retain their individuality and foster their unique talents. That ability to adapt to changing times and challenges is a hallmark of the success of the order.

In recent years, the Jesuits have worked closely with a growing number of volunteers, laypeople attracted by Ignatian spirituality and drawn to work in various Jesuit projects, especially in the area of social justice.

Since Jesuits make a promise not to seek promotion within the Church, it is rare to find Jesuits in senior ranks of the clergy. This vow, however, also entails accepting such positions when required by Church authorities. At the time of his election to the papacy, Jorge Bergoglio was one of six living Jesuit cardinals. Over almost five hundred years, there had been some 500 cardinals chosen from the Society of Jesus.

When he was in the seminary, Bergoglio's grandmother Rosa told him never to forget that he was going to be a priest. The most important thing for a priest, she said, is to celebrate the Mass. She told him of a mother who said to her son, 'celebrate the Mass as if it was your first and your last Mass.' The thought remained with him and inspired him.

The Jesuit training lasts between eight and fourteen years, depending on the previous educational achievements of the novice. During the novitiate in Chile, the main emphasis was on the study of Ignatian spirituality and the experience of the full 30 day Spiritual Exercises. In addition to this, Bergoglio and his companions would have studied Latin, Greek, History and literature. On 12 March 1960, Jorge Bergoglio and his companions took the first vows of poverty, chastity and obedience. Full profession was still thirteen years away for the young Bergoglio.

As the Jesuit Order has a special care for the young and their education, Jorge was assigned to teach literature and psychology at the Colegio de la Immaculada, a secondary school in Santa Fé. He taught the courses between 1964–5 before moving to the Colegio del Salvador in Buenos Aires in 1966. Bergoglio was surprised when his superiors assigned him to teach humanities at the school run by the order. Since he had graduated in chemistry, he had expected to teach the subject. While he found basic psychology easy to teach, the course on literature presented problems.

Although he had developed a passion for literature, his students were less enthused. A meticulous teacher, he nonetheless found it difficult to engage the class. With patience, he learned the art of leading them to knowledge. Many of his students recall his self-discipline and his strictness. However, as he often remarked in later life, education is not simply about mastering subjects. It is also learning about ethical values. This is a hallmark of the Jesuit educational system. Noting that teachers are often underpaid to teach overcrowded classes, Bergoglio urged parents, children, teachers, institutions and governmental bodies to co-ordinate their approach.

Jorge Bergoglio was ordained on 13 December 1969, four days before his 33rd birthday, by Archbishop Ramón José Castellano. His mother, siblings and members of his family attended the ceremony which was followed by a reception for all the newly-ordained priests. A number of his school teachers were also guests.

Immediately following his ordination, Jorge concluded his studies at San José seminary before he and some companions were sent to Madrid, to continue their formation within the Society, at the Jesuit house associated with the University of Alcalá de Henares de Madrid. This period is known within the order as 'tertianship,' and is a spiritual formation. During their time, Jorge and his companions had the opportunity of visiting the town with this prestigious college. Situated 35 km north east of Madrid, the town of some 200,000 inhabitants retains its medieval feel. The college was founded by Francisco Jiménez de Cisneros, who obtained a papal bull from Pope Alexander VI.

This was Jorge's first visit to Europe, the continent of his ancestors. The Church was still in the first flush of enthusiasm caused by the Second Vatican Council. Convened by Pope John XXIII, the Second Vatican Council was the first global gathering of the Church's bishops in almost a century. Over the course of sixteen centuries, twenty ecumenical Councils had discussed issues pertaining to Christian life. Held in major sessions and smaller working commissions between 1962–5, the bishops discussed issues facing the contemporary Church.

They sought methods to make the Christian message adaptable to the world, less than two decades after the Second World War, and during the era of the Cold War. The bishops tried to establish closer links between other Christians and members of the world's faiths. The Council dealt with a number of internal issues. How missionary work was to continue, the role of the laity in the Church, the nature of the ordained ministry and the language and celebration of the sacraments. The Council also discussed improvements in Catholic education and development in social issues.

In 1968, three years after the end of the Council, Pope Paul VI issued a document on the dignity of life (*Humanae Vitae*). Among the issues was a general prohibition on artificial contraception. Many clergy expected a change in the law on obligatory celibacy, even though the bishops had not indicated waiving of the rule.

The post-Conciliar years were filled with hope and frustration, renewed energy and optimism, as well as disillusionment. These were the years in which Jorge Bergoglio and his companions were ordained and began their ministry.

In 1972, Jorge returned to Argentina to take charge of the Jesuit novitiate at Villa Barilari in San Miguel. On 22 April 1973 Father Jorge Bergoglio made his perpetual profession. He was now a fully-formed Jesuit. He was appointed rector of the Colegio Máximo there and lecturer in the Faculty of Theology. At the same time he was named a consultor for the Province of the Jesuits.

However, these appointments were to be short-lived for on 13 July 1973, the Jesuit General appointed Bergoglio as the new Provincial. Although he had made his final vows just four months earlier, Bergoglio was nominated Provincial for a six-year term. It was a surprise to Bergoglio and to the members of the Argentinian Province.

The Jesuit province at the time consisted of 15 houses, 166 priests, 32 brothers and 20 students. The Jesuit Order is governed from Rome by the Superior General and a council of advisors. Globally the order is divided into provinces, each overseen by a Provincial. Assisted by a *socius*, or general advisor, the Provincial oversees the Jesuits in his territory, appointing rectors to houses and directors for colleges and other apostolates. The Provincial acts as a local link between the General based in Rome and the members of the order in a particular country or territory. As Provincial Jorge travelled regularly to the various schools, religious houses and social projects run by the Jesuits throughout Argentina.

The second three years of Bergoglio's period in office coincided with the most brutal period of civil unrest which engulfed Argentina.

In the decades following the Second World War, several countries in South America were caught up in the so-called Cold War. The clash between Communist and Capitalist ideologies in the region led to the establishment of right-wing dictatorships. Some of these were granted military and financial support from the United States of America. Specifically, the Americans were determined to keep Soviet influence from infiltrating the United States.

The 20th century saw six military coups in Argentina. The first was in 1930 and the last took place in 1976. Fourteen dictators were imposed between 1930 and the end of the dictatorship in 1983. Following the 1976 coup, which overthrew President Isabel Perón, General Jorge Videla became de facto President of Argentina, at the head of a military junta.

Videla was determined to destroy both leftist and right-wing groups which used violent methods against the government. The People's Revolutionary Army was the armed wing of the Worker's Revolutionary Party. The Montonero Perónista Movement was a leftist guerilla group, determined to undermine fascist governments by terror and violence.

Many of the members were recruited from Catholic universities and other Church groups. They saw the violence as an unavoidable part of the class struggle which would eventually win freedom and respect for human rights. In 1970, the Montoneros had kidnapped and executed Pedro Aramburo, the dictator who had ruled between 1955–8. In 1972, the group planted a bomb at the Sheraton Hotel. The following year, Colonel Héctor

Irabarren was killed while resisting a kidnap attempt. The Montoneros encouraged Juan Perón to return from his 17-year exile in Madrid to lead the country once more. When Perón returned to Argentina, the group was split over his policies. With Perón's death in 1974, Isabel took over the leadership of the country. She was unable to stop the violence and killings which multiplied during her presidency. Isabel Perón signed laws allowing Videla to act decisively to destroy the opposition.

While combatting the Marxist-inspired groups, the government was supported by the Argentine Anti-communist Alliance, founded in 1973 and led by José López Rega. The right-wing party sought to do away with all opposition to the governing powers, eliminating journalists, leftist guerrillas, union leaders, students, intellectuals, nuns and priests engaged with the poor and all other dissidents. During the period of unrest, many priests and nuns became engaged in the struggle to obtain human rights for the dispossessed, the poorly educated, the unemployed and the disenfranchised.

Despite the natural resources of South America and the Caribbean islands, poverty is an inescapable reality. Centuries of exploitation by Spain and Portugal in the slave trade, corrupt foreign administrators and incompetent rulers reduced much of the population to poverty. Contemporary Argentina has suffered from decades of military and democratically-elected rulers who have failed to advance the nation's prosperity and take advantage of its riches.

During the 1960s and 1970s, corresponding to the political upheaval, some church leaders began to challenge the status quo. They protested against the exploitation of the poor and examined the structures which both led them into poverty and disenfranchised them.

A number of writers emerged, reaching an ever-widening audience and informing them of the injustice of such social structures. One such writer, the Peruvian Dominican priest Gustavo Gutiérrez wrote a number of books arguing that the obligation to eradicate poverty lies with the educated and those who have resources. His seminal work, *A Theology of Liberation* was published in 1971, and immediately gained a wide audience.

Gutiérrez wrote with authority. His mixed ancestry included native Quechua and colonial Spanish blood.

'Poverty is not fate,' Gutiérrez argued, 'it is a condition; it is not a misfortune, it is an injustice. It is the result of social structures and mental and cultural categories, it is linked to the way in which society has been built, in its various manifestations.' Thus Christian engagement with the poor is not a choice, it is an obligation. The Christian is not called to share what is left over but rather to share equally, treating other humans with respect. Above all, it means channelling energies and talents on behalf of the needy. It is Christian solidarity and lies at the heart of the Gospel message.

The bishops of Latin America were deeply aware of the plight of their people although they were divided as to the best manner in which to help. Some bishops tried to create just structures for society, protecting and promoting human rights.

In 1968, the bishops of Latin America met in the Colombian city of Medellín. The Second Vatican Council, which several Latin bishops had attended, had closed three years earlier. The positive energy and enthusiasm which the Council had engendered permeated the meeting at Medellín. The bishops, in a concluding document, identified the 'institutionalised violence' of poverty. They challenged both governments and people to change the political systems which denied the poor access to a basic standard of living, better medical care and the right to work. Although not all the bishops were in favour of provoking governments, the bishops' united statement had an immediate impact.

Four years later, in 1972, the bishops met again. During the meeting they voted the Colombian bishop Alfonso López Trujillo as Secretary General. López Trujillo, who had close connections to the Vatican, convinced several bishops to withdraw their tacit support for the revolutionary theology. The similarity of Karl Marx's analysis of poverty and some theologian's interpretation was seen as too close.

Pope John Paul II travelled to the Mexican city of Puebla in January 1979, to open the Third General Conference of the Latin American bishops. In a lengthy address, he underlined that the Church's main mission is to preach the Gospel. He thinly warned against the developments of recent years:

> People claim to show Jesus as politically committed, as one who fought against Roman oppression and the authorities, and also as one involved in the class struggle. This idea of Christ as a political figure, a revolutionary, as the subversive man from Nazareth, does not tally with the Church's catechesis. By confusing the insidious pretexts of Jesus' accusers with the – very different – attitude of Jesus himself, some people adduce as the cause of his death the outcome of a political conflict, and nothing is said of the Lord's will to deliver himself and of his consciousness of his redemptive mission.

Given John Paul's life under Communist rule in Poland, such caution was understandable. The proponents of liberation theology, however, argued that the world of Latin America was quite different. John Paul had no direct experience of the region and depended on advisors such as López Trujillo, whom he asked to draft the address.

Bergoglio's term of office as Provincial coincided with the development of liberation theology and with the 'dirty war' of the military junta.

Bergoglio, understanding the motivation of his confreres engaged in promoting social justice, took a cautious approach. He urged those under his authority to avoid open conflict with government agents.

Two Jesuit priests, Orlando Yorio and Francisco Jalics were arrested by military police in May 1976. They had asked Archbishop Aramburo and Jorge Bergoglio for permission to live in the favelas while teaching at the university. They were kept illegally, blindfolded and hand-cuffed, and mistreated for five months. During the sessions, the captors told them that Bergoglio had betrayed them. The two believed their kidnappers.

Only in 2000 did one of the priests, Fr Jalics, meet Bergoglio and discuss the issue. Bergoglio tried to convince him that he had actively sought the release of his confreres. On 20 March, seven days after Jorge Bergoglio's election as Pope, Fr Francisco Jalics published a clarification of the events surrounding the kidnapping:

> I myself was once inclined to believe that we were the victims of a denunciation. At the end of the 1990s, after numerous conversations, it became clear to me that this suspicion was unfounded. It is therefore wrong to assert that our capture took place at the initiative of Fr Bergoglio.

Bergoglio himself recalled the events when summoned to a court in 2011. The mandate of the court was to discover the truth about those years.

'I did what I could,' he recalled. 'What was possible for my age, and the few contacts that I had, in order to intercede to have illegally detained persons set free.'

Despite his limited contacts, Bergoglio managed to persuade a military chaplain to allow him to take his place at a celebration Mass attended by the dictator Videla and he used the opportunity to request information about the priests. Other bishops who also pleaded for the 'disappeared,' were equally unsuccessful. After five months the two priests were released.

Bergoglio also hid refugees from the dictatorship at the college. Several fled the country and on one occasion Bergoglio dressed a man who resembled him and gave him his identity card. The period caused a rift between several Jesuits of the province and their Provincial.

In 1980, following his term of office as Provincial, Jorge returned to the academic life as rector of Colegio Máximo de San José, some 30 kilometres south of Buenos Aires. The college was the faculty of philosophy and theology. It was an unusual move for a former Provincial. Jorge had found the six-year term more demanding than he had expected and was glad to move on to another appointment within the order.

In preparation for his new role, Jorge travelled to Ireland where he spent two months (June and July, 1980) living in the Jesuit community at Milltown Park in Dublin. It was partly a sabbatical period but he spent the time learning English with a tutor in the suburb of Clonskeagh.

The following year Regina María, his mother, died, a loss he felt very greatly. He was deeply attached to his mother and although she had not easily accepted his religious vocation, the two had a very close relationship.

Life as rector was tranquil. He enjoyed lecturing but he also served in the parish of San José, in the district of San Miguel. Some saw these years as an exile. Bergoglio recalled them with affection, especially his work in the parish of San José de San Miguel, where he taught catechism. In 1986, Bergoglio finished his term of office. His superiors decided to send him to Germany for six months to prepare for a doctorate. Bergoglio had chosen to work on the contribution of the Italian scholar, Romano Guardini, who had died in 1968.

A highly-regarded philosopher and theologian, Guardini synthesised great thinkers of the past and applied their contribution to contemporary society. He was to have an influence on many of the theologians of the Second Vatican Council. By coincidence, Guardini was to be a great influence on Fr Luigi Giussani, later the founder of the influential religious group, Communion and Liberation. Bergoglio was to become a passionate follower of Giussani's work whose books he read over several decades.

Six months at the Institute of Sankt Georg at Frankfurt proved inconclusive. Failing to choose a subject, Bergoglio returned home to consider another option. In the event, Bergoglio did not proceed with the doctorate as his energies were taken up with the new challenges of guiding the college and his engagement in the establishment of a new parish nearby.

During his time in Germany, Jorge saw a picture which greatly appealed to his imagination. The painting, dating from the beginning of the 18th century, was by the Bavarian artist Johann Georg Schmidtner. The canvas hangs in the church of St Peter am Perlach in Augsburg. It depicts the Blessed Virgin Mary untying knots in a cord. The image was inspired by the writings of third-century writer, St Irenaeus of Lyons. The image so appealed to Jorge that he asked a printer in Argentina to make a copy. It subsequently became enormously popular and, thanks to the efforts of Bergoglio, is venerated throughout Argentina and Brazil.

BISHOP OF BUENOS AIRES

On his return to Argentina in late 1986, Bergoglio was appointed confessor and spiritual director to the Colegio Del Salvador in Córdoba, a role he retained until 1990. He also assisted as a confessor in the nearby Jesuit church. Once more, Bergoglio got involved in the local parish, celebrating Mass, hearing confessions and meeting the people of the district.

The Apostolic Nuncio to Argentina, Archbishop Ubaldo Calabresi, whose lengthy tenure ran from 1981–2000 often consulted Father Bergoglio with regard to candidates for the episcopacy. The Italian-born Calabresi, a native of Sezze Romano, held Bergoglio in high esteem, in particular for his comprehensive knowledge of the clergy of several diocese.

On one occasion, rather than summon Bergoglio to the nunciature in Buenos Aires, Archbishop Calabresi suggested that the two meet at the airport. It would suit the travel plans of both men. Taking the Jesuit aside, the nuncio spoke of several items for which he needed information. As the call was made over the loudspeakers for passengers to board the plane, the nuncio casually remarked; 'Ah, just one more thing. You have been appointed auxiliary bishop of Buenos Aires. The announcement will be made on the 20th of May.'

Father Bergoglio was taken aback by this unexpected news. He recalled later that he literally froze, unable to think how to answer or what to say to halt the news within seven days. In reality, there was little to say or do. Father Bergoglio accepted the task conferred by Pope John Paul II. Obedience to the Pope remains one of the hallmarks of the Jesuit Order.

Preparations were made for the episcopal ordination which took place on 27 June 1992 in the Buenos Aires Metropolitan Cathedral. Cardinal Antonio Quarricino, Archbishop of Buenos Aires was the principal consecrator, assisted by Archbishop Calabresi and Bishop Emilio Ogñénovich. It was Quarricino who had suggested his name to the nuncio.

The new bishop invited his two brothers and sisters, along with other members of the family. A large number of Jesuits attended the ceremony of their former Provincial. Bishop Bergoglio choose as his episcopal motto a line from the writings of the Venerable Bede, a 7th-century monk. In a homily for the feast of St Matthew, Bede wrote:

> *Vidit ergo Jesus publicanum, et quia miserando atque eligendo vidit, ait illi. 'Sequere me'.* [Jesus therefore sees the tax collector, and since he sees by having mercy and by choosing, he says to him, 'follow me'.]

Christianity came to Latin America at the end of the 15th century, following the commercial voyages made by European explorers. Conversion to Catholicism was rapid among those who came in contact with the European conquerers. The reasons were varied. While some converted by conviction, a large number were forcibly baptised by the Spanish and Portuguese friars who settled in the New World and founded missions. For many Europeans, the Americas were a lucrative source of material for the slave trade.

During the early decades of colonial settlement, the Church offered little criticism of the Spanish and Portuguese overlords who took advantage of the riches of the new countries. Many indeed cooperated with the massive exploitation of hundreds and thousands who were sold into slavery. There were significant exceptions, such as the efforts made by the Dominican friar Bartolomé de las Casas. For some 50 years, de las Casas vigorously defended the rights of the indigenous population who were exploited by Spanish slave-traders. Another Dominican friar, Francisco de Vitoria (1483–1546) also defended the rights of the indigenous Indians against the encroachments of Spanish slave-traders.

The first traces of settlement in Buenos Aires date to the mid-16th century when the Spanish explorers led by Pedro de Mendoza set up a village in 1536. This was abandoned five years later in 1541 and lay desolate until the Spanish conquistador Juan de Garay refounded the town in 1580. Henceforth it would be known as the town of the Most Holy Trinity and the Port of Holy Mary of the Fair Winds. Gradually the city became an important port for Spanish traders and expanded.

The diocese of Buenos Aires was erected on 6 April 1620, with the appointment of the first bishop, Fray Pedro Carranza (1621–32). The new diocesan territory was divided from the nearby diocese of Paraguay. A native of the Spanish city of Seville and a member of the Carmelite Order, Bishop Pedro encouraged clergy to come from Spain and work in the new diocese. The bishop recounted that the diocese numbered little more than one hundred houses, not including the population which worked on the plantations. With encouragement from the king of Spain, a number of clerics crossed the Atlantic to help the diocese flourish.

In 1776, the Viceroyalty of the River Plate was established from that of Peru. This territory was the last of the districts loyal to the Spanish crown. By the early 19th century, the people of the viceroyalty sought independence from Spain. Incursions by the British navy in 1806 led indirectly to the War of Independence.

In May 1810, the people of Buenos Aires rebelled against the Spanish authorities which administered the city. The Spanish monarch Ferdinand VII had been deposed two years earlier by Napoleon. In late 1810, Paraguay declared independence.

In 1815, King Ferdinand was restored to the throne. His immediate difficulties lay in securing his grasp of power in Spain; the colonies would have to await his consideration. During the interregnum and early months of the restoration of power, the locals attempted to establish their independence. On 9 July 1816, politicians met at Tucumán, some 1,300 kilometres north of Buenos Aires. Here they declared the independence of the United Provinces of South America from Spanish rule. On 5 March 1866, Buenos Aires was elevated to the status of an archdiocese, comprising parts of Parana, La Plata, Montevideo and Viedma.

In the intervening centuries, the diocese was cared for by both Spanish and native Argentinian clergy. By the election of Jorge Bergoglio to the papacy in 2013, the diocese had grown to an area of more than 200 km² with a population of more than two and a half million Catholics.

The challenge of working as a bishop in this multi-cultural city was immense. A native of the city, Bergoglio was aware of the inequality of the citizens. While some lived in considerable luxury, there were enormous numbers whose lives were stunted by poverty. In a sign of solidarity with the poorer areas, Jorge Bergoglio gave his first interview as a bishop to a parish newsletter, *La Estrella de Belén.*

For administrative purposes, the diocese of Buenos Aires is divided into four zones, Flores, Devoto, Belgrano and Centro, originally satellite towns which lay around the city of Buenos Aires. Bishop Bergoglio was immediately appointed Episcopal Vicar of the Flores district and on 21 December 1993 he was also entrusted with the office of Vicar General of the Archdiocese.

The modern city of Buenos Aires lies on the estuary of the de la Plata River and is one of the 20 largest cities in the world. The population of the Greater Buenos Aires area comprises of some thirteen million people.

For the new bishop, the challenge was to find a method of connecting people with the Church. Decades of the dictatorship had disillusioned thousands of Argentinians, who no longer trusted the Church. During the various coups, the bishops had generally kept silent with regard to the rape, torture and kidnapping in which thousands of citizens died. If his term as bishop was to be fruitful, the challenge lay in presenting the Christian faith in an attractive manner.

Initially, Bishop Bergoglio moved into a Jesuit house in Buenos Aires. Used to living in community for so much of his life, Bergoglio preferred not to live in the spacious residence offered to him by the diocese.

The experience was not universally harmonious. Some of his companions disliked having their former Provincial living among them as a bishop. There was a suspicion among a few that, although now a diocesan bishop, he was meddling in the internal affairs of the order. Others had unfavourable memories of his time as Provincial of the order. There were tensions in the house and some felt that the bishop should leave.

From the beginning, Jorge threw himself into his work. Auxiliary bishops carry out the duties assigned to them by the archbishop, but Bergoglio took the initiative to visit the district of which he was in charge. He met with the clergy of his area and offered them whatever assistance he could.

His style was markedly different from previous bishops. He consulted and listened, even if the responsibility for decisions ultimately lay with him.

The slum areas in the periphery were the first focus of his attention. He urged the wealthier parishes to dispose of some of their resources to help the needy parishes in the shanty towns where houses were made of brick, cardboard and tin.

In 1990, Bergoglio had come into contact with a group of volunteers of 'Puntos Corazón', the Heart's Home, a charitable organisation founded by a French priest, Thierry de Roucy. Bergoglio was impressed by the dedication of the lay workers who went to live in poor areas in order to help those living with difficulties. De Roucy encouraged the volunteers to be kind to the lonely and do whatever was possible to help them. De Roucy did not advocate building structures. It was often sufficient to visit people in their homes and offer simple but effective help and companionship. Bergoglio was impressed by the compassion of the volunteers, most of whom give up more than a year of their lives to help people in difficulty in many countries throughout the world.

As bishop and later as Cardinal Archbishop, Jorge Bergoglio needed to inspire both the diocesan clergy and the members or religious orders. He claimed on more than one occasion that his priests were his parish. If he looked after them, they would work well with and for the parishioners. With only 850 priests in an expanding diocese of two and a half million Catholics, he needed to care for each and every one. He continuously encouraged them to look after their health and when in difficulty, to come to him for help. He also kept contact with the members of religious orders who helped administer a number of parishes, oratories and shrines.

Written correspondence was also attended to as soon as was practical. In his pocket he carried a small notebook. While blessed with a good memory, he nonetheless noted down any requests or requirements to attend to when he returned home.

Although he established a good rapport with his priests, he was also demanding. If he noted that one was not doing his fair share of pastoral work, he would let him know. Bergoglio was also fair – he arranged for priests in difficulty to have counselling and offered financial support.

In *The Jesuit*, a book-length interview given to journalists Sergio Rubin and Francesca Ambrogetti in 2010, Cardinal Bergoglio recalled how a wise priest noted that most priests are happy to have 99 sheep in the fold and fail to go after the one missing. The task of the priest, rather, is to leave the pen in the care of others and search for the lost one.

Good parish structures are important. Often, he lamented, priests are busy with administrative tasks which are not their business but rather should be attended to by the people in the parish. This is more urgent in view of the declining practice rate in Argentina.

Bergoglio was one of three other auxiliary bishops tasked with caring for the diocese. Cardinal Guerricino established a good working relationship with his new assistant. 'I know where Bishop Bergoglio is, even if I don't see him,' he joked at meetings of the bishops. Bergoglio was always in the last row. With his ready smile the new bishop sought to put people at their ease. He insisted on being called Father rather than any greater ecclesiastical title.

Although entitled to a car, Bergoglio preferred to use public transport, either the bus or metropolitan underground. Usually people did not pay attention, but it was an important way for him to keep in contact with his fellow citizens.

On 3 June 1997, Pope John Paul II appointed Bishop Bergoglio as coadjutor to the elderly Cardinal Quarricino. The promotion indicated that Bergoglio would replace Quarricino on the latter's retirement. It was Quarricino who had suggested to the Pope that Bergoglio would be a suitable successor.

On 28 February 1998, the cardinal died and Bergoglio automatically became the Archbishop and Metropolitan of Buenos Aires. Six months later, on 6 November, he was appointed by Pope John Paul II as the Ordinary for the large population of Eastern Rite Catholics who lacked their own bishop. In late June, Archbishop Bergoglio travelled to Rome to receive the pallium, the role of office for Metropolitans. The archbishop went unaccompanied to the ceremony which took place on 28 June.

The Pope had come to know Bergoglio and admired both his way of life and his fidelity to orthodox doctrine. Bergoglio's appointment to one of the largest dioceses in Latin America was a mark of papal esteem.

As the new archbishop, Bergoglio was entitled to move into the grandiose official residence. Protesting that he had been used to living in one room since he entered the Jesuits, he opted to live in a small single bedroom apartment close to the curial offices. This had been a retirement apartment for the elderly Bishop Ogñénovich, formerly custodian of the shrine of Our Lady of Luján. Living by himself, cooking his own meals gave him independence.

The furnishings of the apartment were sparse. The bed had been inherited from his grandparents Giovanni and Rosa. Over the head of the bed hung a crucifix. A picture of Mary, Joseph and Jesus, which had belonged to his family, also hung on the wall. The small wardrobe contained the few clothes he wore. Once a week a lady came to tidy the small apartment and care for the laundry.

In the adjacent room was a study, filled with books. A lamp and a phone sat on the small desk with a diary and phone directory. On the desk and bookshelves were several photographs sent by people he met in the slums. From the studio opened a small kitchen. At lunch the archbishop preferred to eat a light snack, avoiding luncheon invitations.

As bishop, Bergoglio maintained the habit of years in Jesuit communities. Each morning he rose before 5.00 a.m. The early hours of the morning were for prayer in his small chapel and study. While the day was full of appointments, visits and activities, the evening was mostly reserved for his meal and a few phone calls to family and friends. For recreation he listened to the radio and retired early most evenings. On one occasion he received a gift of some CDs. He later asked a friend to record them to cassettes, as he did not have a CD player.

When he became Archbishop, Jorge Bergoglio installed a special phone line for the priests. He gave them the confidential number. If they were in trouble or needed help in any manner, he asked them to call him. To ensure his availability, he gave the hour each morning between 7 and 8 when he would answer the phone personally. There would be no intermediaries and each request for advice or help would be dealt with immediately.

In the diocesan offices he had the assistance of secretaries and staff. The diocese runs several ministries for migrants, the poor, the sick, youths and the elderly. These are delegated to a number of administrators all of whom answer to the archbishop. Given the large size of the diocese, Bergoglio was assisted by six auxiliary bishops. They all met every fortnight in the diocesan offices and discussed the pastoral care of the people.

Shortly after he became archbishop, Jorge Bergoglio established a commission to examine the financial situation of the archdiocese. A scandal had broken out following the arrest of Monsignor Roberto Toledo, the Vicar General, and former private secretary of Cardinal Quarracino in 1997. Other people were also questioned, including Juan Miguel Trusso the son of a former Argentinian ambassador to the Holy See.

The arrest of Toledo by the financial police was connected to the failed Banco de Crédito Provincial and charges of corruption. The police had been alerted to irregularities and in December 1998, the police demanded to examine the archives of the deceased Cardinal Quarracino. Bergoglio countered by contesting that the Argentinian Central Bank had failed its duty in exposing investors in the Banco de Crédito Provincial. A court case was initiated to defend the Church from unjust charges.

The report of the cardinal's commission recommended transferring diocesan accounts from local banks into the larger international banks such as HSBC and UBS, which would lessen the exposure of the diocese in the event of financial collapse. Bergoglio restructured the financial administration of the diocese, insisting on meticulous accountancy and transparency.

On 21 February 2001, Archbishop Bergoglio was created a cardinal in a consistory which took place at the Vatican. Learning of his promotion, Bergoglio requested the many people who wanted to accompany him to the ceremony in Rome to remain at home and donate the money to the poor. When the Argentinian Embassy to the Holy See in Rome offered a dinner and reception for the new cardinal, Bergoglio declined at first. He was finally persuaded when told that his refusal would cause offence to Argentinians in Rome and those who wanted to offer personal good wishes.

As a Jesuit, Bergoglio had taken a vow never to seek high office in the Church. Now he joined the some five hundred Jesuits who had been elevated to the College of Cardinals in five centuries.

When he went to Rome, he traveled with his sister, María Elena. She recalled how they met another bishop who asked if he had managed to get a car from the Vatican to transport them around the city. 'It is all taken care of,' replied the cardinal-elect. It was not quite true, for they trudged on foot throughout the streets of Rome. 'And,' she added, 'for him it was not easy, with his flat feet which always give him trouble.'

On the morning he was to be created cardinal, Father Guillermo Marcó called by the Casa del Clero, to meet the cardinal elect. Marcó had assisted the archbishop unofficially since dealing with the press following the financial scandal of 1998. The two had agreed to meet and travel together to the Vatican, a little over a mile away.

When the cardinal emerged from the residence, Marcó looked around for the official car. 'How are we travelling?' he asked politely. 'What do you mean?' came the reply. 'We are going to walk.' The young cleric was slightly embarrassed as he walked along the street with Bergoglio dressed in bright scarlet robes. All the more so when they stopped in a bar for a coffee on the way. Seeing his companion's discomfort, Bergoglio laughed. 'Don't worry! In Rome you can walk around with a banana on your head and nobody will notice!'

It is tradition to assign to a cardinal a titular church, recalling that the office of cardinalate was originally a parish priest of Rome. Bergoglio was designated the Church of St Robert Bellarmine, a church in the fashionable Parioli district of Rome. The church bore the name of the famous sixteenth-century Jesuit archbishop and post-Tridentine theologian who in two conclaves had declined the papacy.

Jorge took advantage of the visit to Italy to retrace his roots in northern Italy. Travelling to Turin with his sister, he met his relatives in Portacomaro. The mayor authorised a civic reception which the cardinal attended and he received an honour from the town. There was great excitement among the hundred or so members of the Bergoglio family who still lived in the area.

For Jorge and María Elena, it was an emotional visit. In the company of some relatives, they went to see the house where their father had been born and grew up. Although it had been sold since 1929, the new owners showed the Argentinian visitors the house and property. Brother and sister walked arm in arm through the small fields among the grapevines and olive trees. When he left, one of his relatives gave him a small bag. 'This is some of your native soil,' he said. 'Bring it back with you to Argentina and remember where you come from.'

The attack on the Twin Towers in New York and the Pentagon in Washington on 11 September 2001 caused reverberations throughout the world. Three hijacked planes crashed into buildings which killed both passengers aboard and several thousands working in the buildings. When a terrorist group, Al Quaeda, claimed responsibility for the attacks, America and her allies prepared an offensive to destroy them and their supporters.

In the aftermath of the 11 September attacks, there was much talk about the clash of civilisations, between East and West and between Islamic fundamentalists and Christian and post-Christian citizens.

At the Vatican, preparations were underway for the Synod of Bishops. The assembly of senior bishops from all over the world takes place with the pope every two or three years. Established in 1965, the Synod was one of the first fruits of the Second Vatican Council (1962–5). The Synod was designed as a means of allowing the bishops of the church to meet regularly and examine contemporary issues. Although not an executive body, the subjects discussed by the bishops reached a global audience. The theme of the assembly was *The Role of the Bishop in the Third Millennium.*

Given the seriousness of the 9/11 assault Cardinal Edward Egan, Archbishop of New York, stayed in New York. Pope John Paul appointed Cardinal Bergoglio as Adjunct Relator General, or co-chairman of the synod. Since Egan did not attend, the synod was administered by Bergoglio. It was the Argentinian's debut on the international scene.

The Synod took place during the first three weeks of October and Bergoglio oversaw the daily sessions. The participants numbered 252 synodal bishops from 118 countries as well as a number of experts and observers.

Participants recall Bergoglio's stewardship of the Synod as efficient and appreciated the speed with which he dispatched business. With good humour, he was able to cut the speeches of long-winded bishops at the microphone. 'We have to be home by Christmas,' he occasionally joked in his low voice.

The synod gave Bergoglio the opportunity of meeting most of the episcopal delegates and learning of their experiences in their home dioceses. As he listened to their aspirations and problems, he formed a broader idea of the challenges facing bishops throughout the world. They, in their turn, took notice of the softly-spoken prelate, who patiently worked through the vast bureaucracy to bring the final report to the Pope.

John Paul's pontificate was marked by a concern for social justice. During his apostolic journeys throughout the world, he readily criticised policies which he saw as contrary to God's plan. Bergoglio's concern in areas of social and ethical concern was less idealistic as a response to the concrete needs of people.

In 2001, Argentina experienced a dramatic economic crisis. During general elections two years later, the Governor of Santa Cruz province, Néstor Kirchner, won the election when President Carlos Menem withdrew from the presidential race. However, in a low turnout of the electorate, Kirchner had gained only 22 per cent of the votes. In his inauguration speech, the president pledged to improve the declining economy and restore prosperity to the country. Even though Cardinal Bergoglio preferred to lead by example, he was vocally critical of both politicians and citizens who failed to protect the weak in society and he regularly decried the lack of motivation to eradicate poverty.

On the same day of the President's inauguration, the cardinal presided at the annual *Te Deum* celebration to mark National Independence Day. Developing the patriotic theme, Bergoglio called for a just system which would care for the poorest people in the country, criticising 'the invisible dictatorship of real interests, those hidden interests which have taken over the resources and our capacity to evaluate and to think'.

The new president interpreted the cardinal's words as an attack on him and declined to attend further such ceremonies. In reality, Bergoglio always had a strained relationship with politicians, especially those in government. He never missed an opportunity to contribute to debate or criticise.

During his period as Archbishop, Bergoglio was scathing of politicians who failed to improve the economy and social status of the people. Although he rarely issued press releases, he used homilies and sermons to deliver his message. Each year at the Chrism Mass of Holy Thursday he explained to the people and priests his plans for the coming months. These homilies were often read afterwards by politicians for whom Bergoglio was a force with which to be reckoned.

Bergoglio had a pragmatic approach to the administration of his diocese. In an interview with the journalist Stefania Falasca in 2007, Cardinal Bergoglio expressed his 'no-nonsense' approach to the people in the diocese. He had high standards for his clergy. That the archbishop was a Jesuit and not a member of the diocesan presbyterate caused some friction between prelate and clerics. However, Bergoglio challenged the priests to work hard for the people. Rather than wait for them to come to the parish, the priests were to go to the people.

'In Buenos Aires,' Bergoglio noted, 'there are about two thousand metres between one parish and the next. So I said to the priests: "If you can, rent a garage and, if you find some willing layman, let him go there! Let him be with those people a bit, do a little catechesis and even give Communion if they ask him". A parish priest said to me: "But Father, if we do this the people then won't come to church". But why? I asked him: "Do they come to Mass now?" "No", he answered. And so! Coming out of oneself is also coming out from the fenced garden of one's own convictions, considered irremovable, if they risk becoming an obstacle, if they close the horizon that is also of God.'

Bergoglio could be severe with his priests. He poked fun at the pomposity of some clergy. 'I sometimes tell them to look at the peacock. He looks wonderful from the front with shining feathers. But then look at him as he passes from behind, and there you have a different story.'

In the late 1960s and 1970s, a number of priests in Buenos Aires began to work in the shanty towns on the outskirts of the city. According to July 2004 estimates, there are about 640 slums in these areas of suburban Buenos Aires. About 690,000 people live in the crowded areas, packed into 111,000 makeshift dwellings. There is no sanitation and open sewers line the roads.

In May 1968, several priests met together to discuss ways to support the poor people who lived in the slums. This was the era of what is loosely called 'liberation theology'. A year earlier, Pope Paul VI had published a milestone encyclical *Populorum progressio,* concerning the development of the world. In the encyclical, the Pope had stated: 'Nobody is authorised to reserve to his own exclusive use what goes beyond his need, when others lack the necessary.' The pope had urged a solidarity with the poor and challenged the political structures which allow poverty grow relentlessly.

With the tacit support of several bishops, the priests set up a movement, *Movimiento de Sacerdotes para el Tercer Mundo* (Movement of Priests for the Third World). The aim of the clergy was to educate the illiterate and equip youth for employment. They had been inspired by a document which had appeared a year earlier, the *Manifesto of 18 Bishops of the Third World.* This charter had challenged the abuse of political and economical power which deprived vast numbers of humanity basic rights and dignity.

The first priests, numbering a dozen, received permission to work in the villas, the slums of Buenos Aires. Fired with enthusiasm, they built makeshift chapels and fostered the people's devotion to the saints. They also attracted the attention of those who used the people of the district as drug pushers and other petty criminals.

The developments alarmed the government forces, as the priests supported the workers' rights to strike and demand fair pay. The military dictatorship of General Juan Carlos Onganía prohibited these rights. The dictator announced that he would demolish the shanty towns if the people did not desist from political agitation. In December 1969, twenty priests marched on the government offices protesting against the plan. The auxiliary bishop of Buenos Aires, Juan Carlos Aramburo threatened the priests with canonical sanctions unless they desisted from stirring up political unrest.

A year later, however, support for the clergy came from a number of bishops and fellow clerics. Still, many were uneasy with the Leftist politics espoused by several of the more politically-minded clergy. In July 1970, a seminal document was published, the *Declaration of Argentinian Priests*. It stated:

> We are a group of Argentinian priests who, despite our deficiencies, seek to love Jesus Christ, the Church and the Fatherland. We belong to that great part of the Church which seeks to promote the material and spiritual good of people, of the well-off and of the poor. However, we walk an entirely different path from that of Marx, Lenin, Che or Mao.

These were years of global unrest. Bolivia and Argentina were in the throes of political upheaval. War in Vietnam turned into a protracted strife in which the United States was engaged with disasterous results. The 'Priests for the Third World' demanded social change. Some even engaged in an armed struggle. The differences of opinion between members eventually led to the dissolution of the movement in 1976.

Bergoglio strongly supported the priests who volunteered to work in the villas. Although the number of vocations to the priesthood declined during Bergoglio's years as bishop, the number of priests working in the villas more than doubled. Even the newly ordained were encouraged to spend some part of their ministry among the poorest people of the diocese. 'It is not enough to visit the slums,' he told a gathering of clergy, 'we need priests to live with the people there as much as in our other parishes throughout Buenos Aires.'

From the number of candidates who presented themselves to enroll in the seminary each year, only some 40 per cent were chosen. Having spoken to a vocations director, the candidates were invited to spend weekends together before making a decision to study for the priesthood. For some, the priesthood was not a suitable option. For others, the diocese was not the best choice and the vocations director would guide them towards religious orders more in tune with their talents. The archbishop met with the vocations director regularly and attended some of these weekends each year to encourage those thinking of entering the priesthood.

To show his practical support for the priests and the people of the villas, Bergoglio often turned up unannounced to administer baptisms or confirmations. Sometimes it was not possible to contact the priests, where phones did not exist in the shanty towns.

Outside Constitución station, youths from the parish of Santa Elisa and those of the Virgen de Caacupé regularly helped the local clergy. Colourful banners were hung from poles offering baptisms and confessions. The local people often approached the priest for a blessing. Amid the hustle and bustle of the marketplace, Mass was celebrated on the side of the street.

The cardinal also showed his support for priests working in challenging circumstances. Whenever he heard of a priest who was sick or needed a break, he phoned him and offered to substitute for him. The cardinal supported his priests when he knew they were in danger. During the dictatorship, many priests and seminarians were abducted and tortured. At least 18 priests were killed. In the first half of his period in office as Provincial, Bergoglio had experienced the terror and shock of sudden attacks and murders of church personnel.

On 11 May 1974, Fr Carlos Mugica was assassinated outside the church of San Francisco Solano, in the district of Mataderos. The priest was talking to a young couple about their forthcoming wedding when he was gunned down. He was regarded at too close to the Perón faction.

The death of the priest shocked the people who saw him as a martyr. On 9 April 1999 on Bergoglio's instruction, the remains of the priest were disinterred and brought back to the district where he had exercised his ministry. The cardinal celebrated Mass on the occasion, when the remains of the beloved priest were reburied at the Church of Christ the Worker.

In a prayer of reparation, the cardinal expressed the sorrow of the people:

> The death of Father Carlos, for his material killers, for those who were the ideologues of his death, for the complicit silences of most of society and for the times that, as members of the Church, we did not have the courage to denounce his assassination, Lord have mercy.

Today the memory of the handsome, charismatic priest is still venerated by the people whom he motivated and inspired.

In the early morning of 4 July 1976, worshippers arriving for Mass in the church of San Patricio found the doors shut. The church, administered by the Pallotine Fathers, is in the middle-class suburb of Belgrano, in the north of Buenos Aires. A young man, Rolando Savino, offered to climb in a window of the brown-brick church. To his horror, he found the bodies of five men lying in a pool of blood on the ground. On a door near the bodies, which lay face upwards, was scrawled the words:

> *Por los camaradas dinamitados en Seguridad Federal. Venceremos. Viva la Patria.*
> (For the comrades blown up at Federal Security. We will prevail. Long live the Fatherland.)

Close by, on the carpet, appeared the words:

> *Estos zurdos murieron por ser adoctrinadores de mentes vírgenes y son M.S.T.M.*
> (These left-wingers were killed for being indoctrinators of innocent minds and M.S.T.M.)

The anagram referred to the movement of Priests for the Third World.

The people were shocked as the doors were opened and the horror revealed. The three priests of the parish, Alfredo Leaden, 57, Alfredo Dufau, 67, and Alfredo Kelly, 43, had been gunned down. Beside them lay the bodies of two seminarians, Salvador Barbeito, 29, who was rector of the local school and Emilio Barletti, 23.

The massacre shocked the parish and the city. The military condemned the murder of the men, claiming that the work was evidently the work of left-wing guerillas. Twenty police officers had been killed in a bomb explosion two days earlier. It may have been that the execution of the innocent clerics and students was a reprisal killing. In subsequent investigations, it emerged that the military junta had authorised the killing. The papal nuncio, Archbishop Pio Laghi, who had arrived in Buenos Aires on 27 April 1974, was convinced that the military intended to subdue and intimidate Church authorities with such acts of violence. In 1997, Bishop Bergoglio came to the parish to celebrate the Mass marking the anniversary of the massacre.

On 4 July 2001, the 25th anniversary of the killing, he returned to San Patricio to pray for the martyrs. Recalling the victims, Cardinal Bergoglio said,

> I am a witness, because I accompanied Alfie in his spiritual guidance, in his confession, until his death. He only thought of God. And I name him because I am a witness to his heart, and when I mention him I mention all of them.

On 12 April 2006 he led a prayer service in the parish at which President Néstor Kirchner was present. The archdiocese opened the cause for five of the 'disappeared' to be beatified. A year earlier, the remains of Esther Ballestrino de Careaga, who was captured in 1977, were discovered and Bergoglio celebrated Mass at the Church of

Santa Cruz, where she was then interred.

At the end of a Mass celebrated in a villa miseria in 2009, the archbishop told the congregation that one of his priests had received a death threat. It brought back the days of the military junta, but now the assassins were drug barons, not soldiers.

The ever-present scourge of drug pushing and addiction was rampant in the favelas. Along with some lay people, the parish priests in Villa 21 had opened three centres for people who were trying to break their drug habit. This is the largest shanty town among the 24 slums, with about 50,000 people.

A young and idealistic priest who worked in Villa 21, José María 'Pepe' Di Paola, had been stopped by some men and told that he would be shot if he continued to assist the people at the centre. Padre Pepe had opened a refuge in 2008 for young people, providing daily food and education, as well as a social centre for elderly people to meet.

In the past three decades, Argentina, along with other Latin American countries has been ravaged by the illegal drugs industry, in particular paco, a low grade residue of cocaine, left over from the purer drug exported abroad. The drug addicts become entirely disorientated and unable to function. For many people, especially youths, the only refuge is the parish. Here education programmes are developed and efforts are made to find employment for the young people in danger. Often the drug pushers target children to smuggle and sell drugs for them on the streets of the major cities.

An important part of the Church's mission is carried out by catechists. Often volunteers, these catechists assist parents and priests in educating the young people. They organise regular meetings, teaching the children prayers and the Bible. Often they act as social workers, trying to help families weighed by poverty and substance abuse.

When Cardinal Bergoglio visited the slums, he spent time with catechists, encouraging their efforts. Having celebrated Mass, he remained with the parishioners afterwards to share a meal. He insisted on waiting in line to receive his plate with the others. He then sat where he found an empty seat and chatted with the person next to him. It was not unusual for Bergoglio to share a common straw to drink mate, a strong tea popular in Argentina.

Often he would hear of family members in prison. He would take out his black notebook and jot down the names of the loved ones. Within days he would quietly visit the prisons, bringing the greetings of family to the detainees.

Each year in October, Bergoglio celebrated Mass in a sports stadium for the youth of the diocese. The Mass was animated by exuberant young singers and musicians. He preached a short, simple homily. He wisely appointed appropriate priests and catechists to be with the youth, and was available for photographs afterwards.

A man given to spontaneous gesture, it was evident that this came from a genuine care for people. He was willing to change Church practice in order to challenge people's perceptions, celebrating Mass in hospitals and nursing homes. While bishops normally celebrated the liturgies of Holy Week in the cathedral, some also choose to visit parishes of the diocese.

Having celebrated Mass of the Chrism with people and clergy in the morning at the Cathedral, in the afternoon of Holy Thursday, Cardinal Bergoglio celebrated the Mass of the Lord's supper in a city hospital or prison. After the homily, he re-enacted the ceremony of the washing of the feet. For him, the gesture brought the Gospel accounts of the Last Supper to life. He washed and kissed the feet of prisoners, drug addicts, people living with HIV/AIDS, prostitutes and other people living in humiliating situations. He also washed the feet of children and the elderly in the tin-roofed churches of the Villas. While he never carried money on his person, Bergoglio later instructed his secretary to send the families money. These visits were rarely reported in the Argentinian media.

In May 2007, Pope Benedict travelled to Brazil. Central to his pastoral visit was the inauguration of the fifth General Conference of the Bishops of Latin America and the Caribbean over which Cardinal Bergoglio, as president, had asked him to preside.

Speaking at the Marian shrine of Aparecida on 13 May, the pontiff expressed his support for the work of the bishops who served the Catholics of the continent and islands, often in difficult circumstances. Underlying the papal message, however, was a concern for the spiritual haemorrhaging of many Catholics from the faith. Inroads made by Pentecostalists and fundamentalist sects threatened the sacramental life of the Church. The other Christian churches and sects offered an attractive alternative to a stagnant form of Catholicism which was evident in some countries.

Cardinal Bergoglio was one of a small number of bishops who actively engaged with the evangelicals. He was often invited to prayer meetings and services. On one occasion he caused surprise among the evangelicals and consternation among his flock as he knelt in prayer and asked his fellow Christian leaders to pray over him.

The number of Latin American Catholics at the end of the first decade of the 21st century was some 432 million worshipers, three quarters of the entire population. Brazil is the largest Catholic country in the region and in the world, with some 134 million worshippers. However, numbers have declined dramatically from 92 per cent of the population in 1970 to 68 per cent in 2012. Mexico, with 96 million Catholics represents the second largest Catholic population followed by Colombia with 38 million Catholics.

The Catholic population of Argentina is 31 million. The smallest of the Catholic nations are Chile and Ecuador, each with 12 million adherents. The entire region makes up some 42 per cent of the world's Catholics, even if the practice rate is low.

The task of the continent's Church leaders, in a post-missionary period, was to encourage the development of the lay faithful and indigenous vocations. President of the Argentinian Episcopal Conference since 2005, Cardinal Bergoglio played a key part in preparing a dossier for Benedict to read prior to his visit to Latin America. He also assisted in the drafting of the pontiff's speeches and homilies.

Several bishops were apprehensive of Benedict's visit. As Prefect for the Congregation for the Doctrine of the Faith between 1981 until his election as pontiff, Ratzinger showed little sympathy for the Theology of Liberation. Benedict lamented the increase of abortion on the continent, and cautioned against the excesses of both capitalism and Marxism. He urged Catholics to remain faithful to their Church rather than embrace the various new Churches emerging on the continent.

With so many natives of Buenos Aires claiming European ancestry, the city also boasted large communities of the established Christian churches. Bergoglio had a particular affinity for the Orthodox faith, especially appreciating the cult of the Blessed Virgin Mary.

He established close links with the Greek Orthodox Metropolitan Tarasios of Buenos Aires and South America and regularly visited the archbishop and attended church ceremonies. On some occasions, he would attend, simply dressed in his coat, and stand at the back of the church with the people as the Divine Liturgy was performed in the sanctuary.

When Pope Benedict issued a document allowing Anglican converts to Catholicism to form a personal prelature, thus preserving elements of Anglican worship, Bergoglio expressed his exasperation. Speaking with Bishop Gregory Venables, former Anglican Primate in Argentina, he dismissed the pope's gesture in establishing an independent Ordinariate as unhelpful. Although he supported Christian unity, Bergoglio did not interpret this as the best method.

During his time as bishop in Buenos Aires, Bergoglio established a close relationship with the Jewish community, the largest in Latin America. The community had swollen during the period of the Second World War as thousands of German, Polish and Russian Jews sought refuge in South America.

In the early 2000s the archbishop joined a Jewish–Catholic charitable organisation called Tzedaka. The purpose was to help overcome poverty. With Jewish leaders, he often visited the poor districts where Jewish people lived and offered his solidarity. Eleven years after the bombing of the Argentine Israeli Mutual Aid Centre, Bergoglio was the first signatory for a petition to bring the perpetrators to justice and rebuild the complex, later visiting it when it was completed. In 2007, the cardinal was invited to attend a service to celebrate Rosh Hashanah at Benei Tikva Slijot synagogue and offered good wishes for the Jewish New Year.

Having established good relations with Rabbi Abraham Skorka, the two wrote a book, published in 2010 under the title 'On Heaven and Earth.' The two men continued to broadcast a weekly programme on the archdiocesan television station. Cardinal Bergoglio welcomed the opportunity to discuss interfaith relations, noting that

> we succumb as victims of attitudes that don't permit us to have dialogue: arrogance, not knowing how to listen, hostility in our speech, attacking the messenger and so many others. Dialogue is born from an attitude of respect

toward the other person, from a conviction that the other has something good to say.

In December 2012, the Jewish community invited the cardinal to attend the Hanukkah ceremony held in the Temple NCI-Emanu El in Buenos Aires. As a tribute to his steadfast support and friendship with the community in the city, he was invited to light the first flame on the menorah.

The cardinal also fostered relations between Catholics and other faiths. In September 2006, Pope Benedict XVI gave a speech at Regensburg University. Many Muslims were offended by a quotation used by the pontiff concerning the Prophet Muhammad. In the verbal melee which ensued, relations between the Holy See and some Muslim authorities were strained. Bergoglio allowed a service to take place in the Cathedral, in which Muslims and Catholics prayed that the difficulties could be resolved. In order not to offend Pope Benedict, he did not attend.

As he built up relationships with the Muslim community in Buenos Aires, he visited the At-Tauhid Mosque located in the neighborhood of Floresta and the Arab–Argentine Ali Ibn Abi Talib School.

On several occasions he was a guest of the Islamic Centre of the Republic of Argentina and regularly invited religious representatives to dinner at the Archbishop's residence. In November 2012, Muslims, Jews and Christians prayed together in the Cathedral, underlying their joint spiritual union. For this, he was criticised by many who opposed the common prayer of Christians and non-Christians in churches.

Cardinal Bergoglio was critical of 'unjust economic structures' that give rise to great inequalities. Speaking in 2009, he claimed that 'unfair social debt is immoral, unjust and illegitimate.' Argentina was not exempt from criticism and he urged everyone to work to change the structural causes and personal or corporate attitudes that give rise to this situation (of poverty), and through dialogue reach agreements that allow us to transform this painful reality we refer to when we speak about social debt.

For that reason he urged political bodies, financial institutions, industries, trade unions, churches and various charitable and social institutions to cooperate to help poor people free themselves from the barriers to charity.

During the early years of the third millennium, the state's attitude toward many ethical questions was modified. In 1994, President Carlos Menem had declared his opposition to legalised abortion and instituted an annual Day for Life on 25 March. When Néstor Kirchner took office in 2003, government policies changed. According to a survey published in 2007 by the Ministry of Health, the number of abortions each year ranges from 460,000 to 615,000. The president determined to introduce legislation surrounding the practice.

The bishops of the country opposed such developments. The bishops of Latin American and the Caribbean addressed the issue of abortion in a document published in 2007. Speaking at the launch of the document on 2 October of that year, Cardinal Bergoglio lamented the low value which is placed on human life. 'The Church,' he asserted, 'is very conscious of the fact that the cheapest thing in Latin America, the thing with the lowest price, is life.'

Bergoglio was pragmatic about 'sex-education' aimed at the appropriate age groups. The key to such formation, he argued, is respect for the human person, aimed at the 'age and receptivity of the young people'.

The cardinal continued to oppose abortion and urged women to carry their pregnancies to term. In a speech in 2012, he asserted that 'abortion is never a solution. We listen, support and offer understanding from our place to save two lives: respect the human being small and helpless, they [doctors] can take steps to preserve your life, allow birth and then be creative in the search for ways to bring it to its full development.'

The cardinal expressed indignation when he heard that some priests refused to baptise children whose parents were not married.

> In our ecclesiastical region there are priests who don't baptise the children of single mothers because they weren't conceived in the sanctity of marriage. These are today's hypocrites! Those who clericalise the Church. Those who separate the people of God from salvation. And this poor girl who, rather than returning the child to sender, had the courage to carry it into the world, must wander from parish to parish so that it's baptised!

On another occasion, in an interview with the journalist Gianni Valente in the magazine *30 Days*, Cardinal Bergoglio recalled how he had met a woman during a visit to a parish, to celebrate the feast of San Cayetano. She told him that she had seven children with two different fathers. Working as a maid, she didn't have enough money to pay for a party, or to invite all fourteen godparents to celebrate the christening.

The cardinal suggested a solution. If she was worried she could not gather all fourteen godparents together, she could ask just two to represent the others. He invited her to bring the godparents and children to the chapel at his residence, where he baptised all seven. After the private ceremony where the children were baptised, the cardinal provided refreshments, sandwiches, cakes and soft drinks for the guests. When she was leaving, the mother thanked him for making her feel special, to which he replied, 'Señora, where do I come in? It is Jesus who makes you important.'

As archbishop of one of Latin America's premier cities, Bergoglio's words were listened to with special interest. He generally avoided giving interviews. 'It's not my strong point,' he insisted to journalists who constantly requested his comment on various subjects. Although a shrewd man, he felt unable to avoid the pitfalls which lay around the field of interviews. His major interview, later published as *El Jesuita*, was given to the two journalists who had gained his trust. A shy man with regard to himself, Jorge Bergoglio revealed his sense of humour, his wit, his sarcasm, determination and depth of conviction.

Bergoglio was aware of the importance of the media. His friendship with Rabbi Skorka and the conversations were unique in Latin America. The dialogue between a Jewish and Christian leader provided an opportunity for each to explain to the other the intricacies of their respective faiths. They built up mutual trust and thus were able to pose difficult questions to each other.

The rule of celibacy for Latin-rite priests is a constant source of discussion and debate. Recalling a period when he was a seminarian and developed a liking for a girl he met at an uncle's wedding, Bergoglio confessed that he was confused. Should he leave his religious vocation and follow her? He realised that such thoughts were entirely normal. For a long time, he told Rabbi Skorka, he struggled with the desire to leave and explore a relationship with the girl, or remain in the seminary. After much soul-searching, he resolved to pursue his studies for the priesthood.

Bergoglio underlined his favour of celibacy, but agreed that it was a theme in need of discussion. If the law of celibacy is relaxed, Bergoglio believed, it would be done on a regional basis, according to cultural demands, rather than a universal abolition of the requirement. This view of gradualness is a hallmark of his intellectual make up, which has also made him a formidable negotiator.

Bergoglio did not talk about celibacy in a vacuum. Apart from his personal experience, he dealt with many priests and even a bishop who broke their vows. In particular, he was unique among the county's bishops in the kindness he showed toward a bishop who had resigned from his diocese and married.

Jerónimo Podestá, born in 1920, was a native of Ramos Mejía, the same district of Buenos Aires in which Bergoglio had been born. In 1962, he was consecrated a bishop and appointed to head the nearby diocese of Avellaneda-Lanús. He participated in the three sessions of the Second Vatican Council and was enthused by the discussions and debates in Rome. Podestá had a charismatic personality and worked to improve the conditions of the poor in his diocese.

In 1966, Podestá fell in love with his secretary, Clelia Luro, a mother of six children. The nuncio, Archbishop Umberto Mozzioni heard of the affair and requested him to end it or resign as bishop. Podestá refused to end the affair and was forced to resign. In 1972 he was laicised and married Luro. Two years later, he was exiled by the Alianza Anticomunista Argentina, the right-wing party, which found his politically progressive views unacceptable.

Podestá and his wife settled briefly in several cities, Paris, Mexico City, Rome and also in Peru before he was allowed return to Argentina when the dictatorship collapsed in 1983. By now, Podestá was largely forgotten. The scandal of the era had passed. He and Clelia lived in penury with no church pension to support them.

Clelia publicly acknowledged the kindness and attention she and her husband received from Bergoglio. When Podestá died, his widow wrote to him on a weekly basis. As soon as he received the letter he phoned her to see how she was. After Podestá's death, Bergoglio was the only one to offer public support to her and he also arranged for financial assistance.

While he was the first bishop to regularly visit the slum areas of his diocese, Bergoglio was attentive to all the parishes, accepting invitations to celebrate the sacraments and join in the life of the parish. When he visited parishes, he always celebrated Mass with the people. Whether a beautiful church in a good part of the city or in a poorer area where a church building did not exist, Bergoglio was happy simply to meet the people of the district.

He developed an easy style of preaching. He encouraged people with anecdotes which evoked an emotional response. 'I am a beggar,' he often remarked. 'I have to beg a lot of things from God. But I like to beg!' He rarely prepared texts, prefering to extemporise. People became used to his informality, his raised eyebrows, his laughs and his intensity.

Archbishop Bergoglio however, had to deal with sensitive issues which pertained both to the Church in Argentina and the global Church. As cases of cover-up were exposed in religious orders and dioceses throughout the world, Jorge Bergoglio was resolute in his views. In his conversations with Rabbi Skorka, Bergoglio addressed the issue of paedophilia. Although he claimed not to have had first-hand experience of instances of paedophilia, he recounted how an American bishop had once asked him for advice. The cardinal was clear:

> I told him to take away the priests' licenses, not to allow them to exercise the priesthood any more, and to begin a canonical trial in that diocese's court. I do not believe in taking positions that uphold a certain corporative spirit in order to avoid damaging the image of the institution. That solution was proposed once in the United States: they proposed switching the priests to a different parish. It is a stupid idea; that way, the priest just takes the problem with

him wherever he goes. The corporate reaction leads to such a result, so I do not agree with those solutions. Recently, there were cases uncovered in Ireland from about twenty years ago, and the present Pope [Benedict XVI] clearly said: 'Zero tolerance for that crime.' I admire the courage and uprightness of Pope Benedict on the subject.

Shortly before he concluded his six-year term of office as President of the Episcopal Conference of Latin America and the Caribbean in 2011, Bergoglio led the bishops of Argentina in a public apology for the supine role some of their colleagues had taken during the Dirty War. Already on 27 April 1996, the Argentinian bishops had issued an oblique apology for 'sons of the Church which responded illegally to the guerillas in a shocking and atrocious way, which brings shame to all'. In 2010, Bergoglio spearheaded a more focused and honest admission that some bishops had failed to stop the massacres carried out by members of the military dictatorship. In some cases, their silence contributed to the tortures and killings.

Another political clash came that same year as the government proposed legalising 'same-sex marriages'. The bishops opposed the intended legislation, arguing that it would change the whole nature and definition of marriage itself. In a letter dated 8 July 2010 to the Carmelite Sisters of Buenos Aires, Cardinal Bergoglio observed:

> It is not a simple political struggle but pretends to destroy God's plan. It is not about a mere bill (this is only the instrument) but a move by the Father of Lies that seeks to confuse and deceive the children of God.

THE FIRST CONCLAVE

On the evening of 2 April 2005, Archbishop Leonardo Sandri announced to the tens of thousands gathered in St Peter's Square that Pope John Paul II had died. A native of Buenos Aires, Sandri occupied the position of Sostituto, the deputy Secretary of State. Having spent most of his life in the diplomatic service of the Holy See, Sandri was the second most important prelate in the Vatican after the pope. It was he who read to the public the last speeches of the Polish pontiff who had been paralysed by Parkinson's Disease.

Karol Wojtyla had been elected on 16 October 1978, following the sudden death of Pope John Paul I after only one month in office. The cardinal had been Archbishop of Krakow since January 1964. The cardinals gathered for that October conclave had been shaken by the demise of the pontiff. Spurred on to elect a younger and more robust pontiff, the cardinal's choose the first non-Italian in five centuries. Taking the name John Paul in honour of his predecessor, the new pope swept onto the world stage with an actor's flair and an athlete's energy. During a pontificate which lasted almost 27 years, he won adoring fans and implacable critics.

As a youth, Wojtyla had lived through the horrors of the Second World War which had engulfed Europe between 1939 and 1945. His own country had been invaded by both German and Russian troops. Human misery, never before experienced on such a savage scale, destroyed the heartland of Europe.

When the war ended, there followed a period of further stagnation and despair. Poland was brought into the orbit of Russian Communism, yet did not lose its fierce nationalism which for centuries had been its proud hallmark. Wojtyla had tried to keep the Christian faith of his people alive during the atheistic Communist rule. He clashed regularly with the national authorities and argued for the freedom of worship for his people. As pope, he brought the same pugnacious style to his pontificate. Surviving an assassination attempt in 1981, John Paul saw his pontificate unfurl in a mystical manner.

John Paul took advantage of improved means of travel to bring the Gospel message to local churches. As he expounded doctrine, he also centralised the Church around Rome. While John Paul had won popular appeal, particularly through a series of 104 international visits, he also evoked fierce opposition to some of his uncompromising teachings on sexual mores and church discipline. John Paul was criticised for his authoritarian manner, his overly-centralised government, his lack of understanding of women's role in the Church and the appointment of conservatives to the episcopate. While he was widely feted, his teaching was largely ignored. Despite his undeniable charm, John Paul did not dialogue with those whose thinking differed from his own.

Ultimately an enigmatic figure, Pope John Paul II had expanded the profile of the papacy enormously.

More than one million mourners filed past the pontiff's corpse as it lay in state in St Peter's Basilica. His funeral, the largest in history, was watched on television by a global audience of close to two billion people. The Patriarch of Constantinople, Bartholomew, attended the papal funeral, the first time such an event had occurred in the history of

Christianity. The unexpected outpouring of grief was accompanied by hysterical calls for him to be canonised immediately.

Following the lengthy pontificate, the cardinals were faced with the dilemma of finding a pope to follow in the shadow of the late pontiff. The method of choosing a new bishop of Rome had a long and varied history. When the apostles decided to replace Judas Iscariot, they drew lots. It was an obscure disciple, Matthias, who was chosen to take the place of Judas. This form of replenishment did not continue. As the apostles died, their place was gradually taken by overseers, or bishops. The evolution of the office took several decades. By the early second century, only one administrator was in charge of an area. The concept of the diocese, a district governed by a bishop, was introduced definitively by the emperor Constantine in the 4th century.

There is little clear information about the election of the bishops in the early church. In the mid-third century, St Cyprian of Carthage observed that bishops were elected by clergy and people, in the presence of neighbouring bishops. Following the death of Liberius, the bishop of Rome in September 366, the people and clergy gathered to elect a successor. Rioting erupted when two deacons, Ursinius and Damasus were elected simultaneously. One hundred and thirty-seven people died before order was restored by the civil authorities.

When the diocese of Milan became vacant in 374, there were divisions among rival groups. The prefect of the city – the equivalent to a mayor – was called to the church where rioting had broken out. The prefect, Ambrose, tried to restore calm. The people began to chant 'Ambrose for bishop.' Although not yet baptised, Ambrose was elected and later received formal approval from the emperor Gratian.

During the 9th and 10th centuries, the papacy was in the hands of a few powerful Roman families. To have a member a cardinal ensured the family's fortunes. In 1059, partly to avoid family factions, the election of a new pope was confined to the College of Cardinals. The assent of the clergy and people was given only after the election. In 1274, the concept of locking the cardinals into a hall was introduced to speed up the process. It followed a papal election at Viterbo which had lasted from November 1268 until September 1272.

In intervening years the election to the papacy saw candidates bribe fellow cardinals to win the throne of St Peter and threaten others. Laws against simony, the buying or selling of ecclesiastical privileges, were introduced. Pope Pius VI died in 1799 as a prisoner of the emperor Napoleon. Some thought the papacy would not survive into the 19th century.

In recent centuries, the papacy has become an office dreaded by most, desired by few. Expectations are high and the stamina and dedication required appears at times to be beyond human capabilities.

While some argued for a return to the practice of the early Church, with a body of electors made up of men and women of various nationalities and attributes, Pope John Paul II had left specific instructions on how the conclave should elect a new pope. All the cardinals were to come to the Vatican following the death of the pontiff to meet in General Congregations between 15 and 20 days after his death. 120 of the cardinals under the age of 80 were to select the new pontiff by ballot. Confined to the Sistine Chapel for a series of votes each morning and afternoon, the election was to proceed until one candidate received a simple majority.

On 18 April 2005, the cardinals and the people of the city of Rome celebrated Mass at St Peter's Basilica. Among the concelebrants was Jorge Bergoglio. This was to be his first time to participate in a conclave.

The Cardinal Dean, Joseph Ratzinger, was the principal celebrant and delivered an analytical homily. Surveying the state of the Church at the beginning of the third millennium, he noted how the barque of Peter seemed continuously buffeted by the winds of change. Noting the various ideologies which developed during the 20th century, he observed,

> Today, having a clear faith based on the Creed of the Church is often labeled as fundamentalism. Whereas relativism, that is, letting oneself be 'tossed here and there, carried about by every wind of doctrine', seems the only attitude that can cope with modern times. We are building a dictatorship of relativism that does not recognise anything as definitive and whose ultimate goal consists solely of one's own ego and desires.

That afternoon the 115 cardinal electors filed into the Sistine Chapel. Ratzinger's words had struck a deep cord with many. Placing their right hand on a copy of the Gospel, each cardinal swore in conscience to elect the one most suitable as successor to Peter.

When Archbishop Piero Marini, Master of Pontifical Ceremonies called *extra omnes* – all leave, the great oak doors of the 15th-century chapel were closed and sealed. The 115 cardinals who entered the conclave came from 50 countries; all but three had been created during John Paul's pontificate. This was the largest number in history to elect a pope.

The first ballot was taken that evening. Although inconclusive, it provided the cardinals with a small number of names from which the new pontiff would be chosen. The ballots were burned in a stove at the rear of the chapel. The cardinals had failed to identify a single candidate. A chemical powder was added to the paper ballots to produce a black smoke. When the burning ballot smoke emerged at 8.04 p.m. through a chimney in the roof, visible from St Peter's Square, the crowds gathered below knew that no pope had been elected.

The cardinals knew that it would be impossible to find a candidate who had attracted global attention in the manner in which the Polish pontiff had done. The challenge was great but the cardinals were anxious not to have a prolonged conclave as this would indicate division to the waiting world.

Although the cardinals were sworn to secrecy and had decided not to speak with the media until the conclave was over, the results of the balloting subsequently became broadly known. A cardinal kept a diary during the two-day conclave and the contents eventually leaked to the Italian press. According to the anonymous cardinal, Cardinal Joseph Ratzinger gained the most votes, followed at a distance by Cardinal Martini, the Jesuit Archbishop of Milan. As Cardinal Martini knew he was suffering from Parkinson's Disease, it is believed that he asked his fellow cardinals not to consider him for office. Some believe he began to push for Bergoglio's election.

On the morning of 19 April, the cardinals met once more in the chapel. The results of the two morning ballots were also inconclusive, but it was clear that Cardinal Ratzinger was approaching a majority. Bergoglio's votes were the next single block, probably numbering at least 40 ballots.

At the first ballot of the afternoon session, Cardinal Ratzinger passed the required 77 votes, obtaining the necessary two thirds majority for a valid election. As the ballots continued to be counted, applause broke out throughout the chapel. The news could now be announced.

At ten minutes before six o' clock, the ballots were burned and the positive result was seen by the crowds in St Peter's Square as the white smoke rose from the chimney. As the crowds cheered at the result, the bells of St Peter's and the city of Rome began to peal.

Presenting himself to the crowds an hour later, the new pope explained he was 'a humble worker in the vineyard of the Lord'. His brief introduction ended with the blessing *urbi et orbi*, to the city and to the world.

THE BENEDICT YEARS

Unlike the unknown Wojtyla, Joseph Ratzinger was a familiar figure in the Vatican. A former professor of theology in several German universities, Joseph Ratzinger had been consecrated Archbishop of Munich on 28 May 1977 and created a cardinal a month later. Following a papal visit to Germany in 1980, Pope John Paul II decided to name Ratzinger as Prefect of the Congregation for the Doctrine of the Faith. While the cardinal initially resisted, he accepted the appointment on 25 November 1981. The Vatican would be home for the rest of his life.

As a theologian, Ratzinger had participated as a *peritus* or expert at the Second Vatican Council. He was seen as progressive, even questioning compulsory celibacy. As Prefect of the Congregation for the Doctrine of the Faith, he took a strict approach to theologians whom he interpreted as liberal or unfaithful to the teaching of the Church. During his period in office, he played a pivotal role in the production of the *General Catechism of the Catholic Church* and a revision of the Code of Canon Law. In 2000, his office also issued a controversial document, *Dominus Iesus* (On the Unicity and Salvific Universality of Jesus Christ and the Church), which many believed caused a setback to Christian unity.

As pope, Benedict defined himself as successor to St Peter. Although he was 77 at the time of his election, he set about following in the footsteps of John Paul II, whose cause for beatification he approved a month after his election, and whom he beatified on 1 May 2011.

Benedict's love of theology and the liturgy permeated his pontificate. His homilies and catechesis were profound and during his pontificate he produced a trilogy on the life of Christ. Softly spoken, he generally followed the programme laid out by John Paul II. An initial attempt to reform the Roman curia was abandoned the year after his election. On 7 July 2007 he allowed the widespread use of the Latin liturgy in use prior to the reforms introduced in the post-Vatican II era. It was a partly unsuccessful attempt to heal the rift between traditionalists attached to the old rite and mainstream Catholics. His lifting of a bar of excommunication on four bishops was severely criticised when one of them, Richard Williamson, controversially denied the horrors of the holocaust of Nazi Germany.

Benedict tried to strengthen the relationship between the Catholic Church and the Jewish faith introduced by Pope John XXIII. Relations with Islam faltered in 2006, when Pope Benedict quoted from an obscure medieval text which declared that the Prophet Mohammed, founder of the Islamic faith, was 'evil and inhuman'. He was delivering a magisterial address at the University of Regensburg, where he had taught theology as a professor. The quotation from a 14th-century document was not understood by Muslims who reacted against the reports of the pontiff's remarks.

Reacting within days to the statements, speaking through a spokesman to Newsweek Argentina, Cardinal Bergoglio distanced himself from the remarks as they were reported.

'Pope Benedict's statement doesn't reflect my own opinions', the Archbishop of Buenos Aires said. 'These statements will serve to destroy in 20 seconds the careful construction of a relationship with Islam that Pope John Paul II built over the last twenty years.' In the event, the pontiff was able to rectify the damaged relationships. Shortly afterwards, inviting prominent Muslim clerics and leaders to meet him at Castel Gandolfo, Benedict apologised for the misunderstanding, while accepting that the quotation was misguided.

Perhaps the greatest shadow over the papacy of Benedict was the scandal of the sexual abuse of children and vulnerable young adults by clerics. Having disciplined the founder of the Legionaries of Christ for abuse, the pontiff sought to heal the deep pain and anger among victims and their families. In a strongly-worded letter to the people of Ireland, Pope Benedict expressed his horror and revulsion while pledging to assist with those who sought to overcome the emotional scarring caused by abuse. Both at the Vatican and on pastoral visits he met victims of the clerical abuse and offered comfort.

In May 2012, a book appeared by an Italian investigative journalist, Gianni Nuzzi. The book, entitled *Your Holiness*, was based on letters and documents stolen from the desk of Pope Benedict and his private secretaries in the papal apartments. Although the journalist protected the thief of the documents, Monsignor Georg Gaenswein recognised a letter which could only be traced to the innermost circle at the Private Apartment. Calling the immediate staff, the pope's butler and four ladies who care for the papal apartment, Gaenswein confronted them with proof that one of them had stolen the documents. Although all denied it, Gaenswein handed the case to the papal gendarmerie, the Vatican's internal police. Following a raid on the apartment of the papal butler, some one thousand documents were found neatly stored in a set of cardboard boxes.

While the 46-year-old butler, Paolo Gabrieli, protested his innocence, it soon became clear that he was the source of the larceny. The journalist refused to cooperate with the police, insisting on the confidentiality of the thief. He indicated that there were several people involved in stealing the documents. For Gabrieli, there was also the embarrassing question of a gold nugget, a cheque made out to Pope Benedict and a valuable antiquarian book. These had also been pilfered from the papal apartment.

International interest was immediate. Media sources saw the events as further proof that the seat of administration for the global population of 1.2 billion people was corrupt. The pressure on the elderly pontiff was immense. Pope Benedict had begun to consider retirement in March 2012, following an exhausting visit to Mexico. More recently he had received a heart pacemaker. As he faced a frail old age and increasing health worries, he took the decision to abdicate. He would be the first reigning pontiff in almost six centuries to retire. Since nobody could accept his resignation, he choose the moment when he could announce his abdication to the cardinals.

Shortly before his birthday on 17 December 2011, Cardinal Jorge Bergoglio submitted his resignation from office to Pope Benedict. The Code of Canon Law requires that diocesan bishops retire at the age of 75. For bishops who are cardinals, retirement is often delayed for a year or two.

Always a well-organised and meticulous man, the cardinal had made adequate preparations. All his papers were in order. A file had been prepared for the successor, whom Bergoglio hoped would be appointed within a year.

For his retirement, the archbishop intended to live in the retirement home for priests of the diocese, which, by happy chance, was in his native district of Flores. He confided his retirement to the auxiliary bishop of Buenos Aires, Eduardo Garcia, offering to help out in parishes which needed assistance and also with spiritual direction for whomsoever requested it. Spiritual discernment was a particular charism of the Jesuit Order.

With his letter submitted, Bergoglio waited patiently for his resignation to be accepted. Friends and colleagues noted that the cardinal did not seem anxious to retire. Several noted that he was morose when he spoke of life in retirement.

THE ABDICATION

On the morning of 11 February 2013, Pope Benedict XVI met with cardinals resident in Rome for a public consistory. The occasion was to proclaim the canonisation of a number of saints and to set the date for the public ceremony. A minor ritual, cardinals from outside Rome rarely travelled to take part. As the ceremony drew to a close, the pontiff added a few words, which he noted, would be important for the life of the Church. This was an understatement.

'After having repeatedly examined my conscience before God,' Benedict said in a low voice, 'I have come to the certainty that my strengths, due to an advanced age, are no longer suited to an adequate exercise of the Petrine ministry.' Several of the cardinals present failed to understand the significance of the words delivered by the pontiff in Latin. Surprised glances were exchanged as the Latin words were slowly interpreted in whispers.

The pontiff explained the decline in mental and physical strength which he had experienced in recent months. 'For this reason,' he declared, 'and well aware of the seriousness of this act, with full freedom I declare that I renounce the ministry of Bishop of Rome, Successor of St Peter, entrusted to me by the cardinals on 19 April 2005, in such a way that as from 28 February 2013, at 8.00 p.m., the See of Rome, the See of St Peter, will be vacant and a conclave to elect the new Supreme Pontiff will have to be convoked.'

The cardinals met the unexpected announcement with surprise and perplexity. None could have foreseen the pontiff's dramatic decision. Not since 1415 had a pontiff resigned. When Pope Gregory XII renounced the papacy, it was in the full flood of the Great Western Schism, a period in which three popes vied for validity. In order to allow a new pope be elected, the three had been forced to abdicate.

The last voluntary abdication had take place in 1294. In August of that year, a lengthy conclave concluded at Perugia when a hermit, Pietro of Morrone, accepted his election as Celestine V. Pietro was a monk, not even a cardinal and he had not been present at the surprise election. His pontificate lasted only four months. The cardinals realised that by not vetting the hermit they had chosen a man with whom they had little in common.

Tales of Pietro's saintly reputation had led them to believe he was a suitable pontiff. However, his rough and uneven Latin and his poor grasp of administration made him the laughing stock of the cardinals. Upon his abdication he was detained at the castle of Fulmone in central Italy where he later died a prisoner,

What Benedict would do in retirement was the subject of enormous speculation. Would he return to his native Bavaria or live in the seminary of Bressanone, where he had spent several holidays as cardinal? Would he retire to an Italian monastery, such as the famous abbey of Montecassino?

In the event, the pope chose to retire to the former gardiner's house in the Vatican Gardens. A community of contemplative nuns had lived and prayed in the converted house since 1994 when they were invited to abide there by Pope John Paul II. The nuns had left the previous October and thus the property could be converted into a suitable residence for the retired Bishop of Rome.

Hearing the news of Benedict's immanent departure, the cardinals prepared to travel to Rome.

On 27 February, Cardinal Bergoglio arrived at Fiumicino Airport. Two other cardinals had arrived at the same time. The Brazilian Cláudio Hummes, the former Archbishop of Sao Paolo, was a Franciscan and had served for six years as Prefect for the Congregation for the Clergy. Cardinal Luis Antonio Tagle of the Philippines was also awaiting his luggage. The two older men offered their congratulations to Tagle, who had been named a cardinal the previous November. The cardinals had come to assist at a farewell audience given by Pope Benedict on the morning of his resignation.

Speaking in the Clementine Hall in the Apostolic Palace, Benedict XVI made his last official speech. It was a fitting end. His first official speech had been in the Sistine Chapel celebrated with the cardinals following his election in 2005. Now, his last words were to the cardinals who would soon gather to elect his successor.

Assuring the cardinals that he would be close to them over the coming days, he prayed that they would be 'completely docile to the action of the Holy Spirit in the election of the new pope'. Importantly, he added that he would also submit to the authority of a new pontiff, whomsoever it should be:

> May the Lord show you the one whom he wants. And among you, in the College of Cardinals, there is also the future pope to whom today I promise my unconditional reverence and obedience.

In order to leave the cardinals entirely free from papal interference, Pope Benedict had decided to withdraw to Castel Gandolfo, the country residence of the popes which had been in use since the 16th century until the former convent had been converted. That afternoon, shortly before 5.00 p.m., Pope Benedict left the papal apartments which he had occupied for little under eight years. As he exited from the elevator, he took his cane in order to steady himself as he walked the final few paces to the Courtyard of St Damasus. His secretary and recently appointed Prefect of the Papal Household, Archbishop Georg Gaenswein, stood behind him, his eyes moist with tears. The Vicar of Rome, Cardinal Agostino Vallini accompanied the pope as he saluted his staff for the last time.

As the pope left the palace, applause fluttered about the small crowd of Vatican personnel who had gained access to the courtyard. His chauffer of several years genuflected to kiss his ring, unable to restrain his tears. Benedict was composed and entered the car for the short journey which would bring him to the heliport, a pad designed in 1976 to allow the pope to leave and enter the Vatican without disrupting Roman traffic. Saluted by Cardinal Sodano, the Dean of the Sacred College at the heliport, Benedict prepared to leave the Vatican for the last time as pope.

Monsignor Leonardo Sapienza, Regent of the Papal Household, explained to the pontiff that the helicopter would do a circle around the cupola of St Peter's so that the pope could make his farewell. The journey lasted barely 15 minutes as the helicopter flew south towards the Alban Hills. The sun had almost set as the pontiff arrived at the villa. He went immediately to the outer facade to greet the crowds which had gathered to bid him farewell.

Addressing the crowd briefly, the pope thanked them for their presence. Acknowledging that this was a day like no other, the pope asked for their prayers.

> I am simply a pilgrim beginning the last leg of his pilgrimage on this earth. But I would still thank you, I would still – with my heart, with my love, with my prayers, with my reflection, and with all my inner strength – like to work for the common good and the good of the Church and of humanity.

At 7.59 p.m., the Swiss Guard withdrew their service of protection for the pope. At 8.00 p.m., the bells at the village Church of St Thomas tolled the end of Benedict's pontificate. A ripple of applause ran through the crowd, as the great oak doors overlooking the square were closed and locked. The pontificate of Benedict XVI was at an end. He had been Pope for seven years and ten months. Most turned away in sadness.

Bergoglio studiously avoided public comments about the forthcoming election, but had told Argentina's daily, *La Nación*, that his age precluded him from election. Convinced that he would be able to leave Rome shortly after the conclave, he had booked his return ticket, economy class, for 23 March.

Shortly before his resignation, Pope Benedict published a *motu proprio*, a short letter concerning the immanent conclave. While Pope John Paul II had decreed in 1996 that 15 to 20 days could elapse following the vacancy of the Holy See, Benedict allowed the cardinals freedom to change the timescale. On 1 March Cardinal Angelo Sodano, the 85-year-old Dean of the College of Cardinals, sent a message summoning the cardinals to Rome. The conclave was to begin immanently.

In order to prepare adequately, the cardinals met over a number of days in General Congregations. All who participated in the conclave had been created by John Paul II or Benedict XVI. Only during the *sede vacante* period do the cardinals experience total freedom to speak openly among themselves without the presence of the pope.

The first congregation took place in the Paul VI Audience Hall on the morning of 4 March. The cardinals decided to meet twice each day, with the exception of Wednesday afternoon, when a prayer service in St Peter's Basilica would replace the second session.

John Paul II had expressed a firm wish that these meetings be confidential, thus giving the cardinals an opportunity to discuss issues openly. Each cardinal was allotted five minutes to make a brief intervention on the state of the Church.

After the morning meetings on Monday and Tuesday, some of the North American cardinals gave press conferences. Speaking candidly about the challenges in the church and the world, the conferences were attended by a large number of journalists.

On Wednesday the press conference was abruptly cancelled as some other cardinals objected to the North American initiative. The only other daily press briefings were offered by the spokesman of the Holy See, the Jesuit Fr Federico Lombardi.

The issues confronting the Church were enormous. The world's population was expanding rapidly, requiring new responses from church leaders to evermore complex issues. Poverty, human rights and sexual mores were among the issues which repeatedly surfaced in the interventions of the cardinals. In many places, notably Europe and Latin America, the numbers of active Christians was on the wane. In some countries, Christians were brutally persecuted. The Church faced both challenges and opportunities.

Many of the problems were internal. The inequality which women faced in the church, the leaked documents from Benedict's office, the accusations of money laundering through Vatican institutions and corruption charges all needed to be examined and resolved. In one of the last interventions at the General Congregation, Cardinal Bergoglio made a brief four-minute intervention. It was short and to the point.

Following the conclave, Cardinal Jaime Ortega, the Archbishop of Havana, revealed how impressed the cardinals had been. He asked the Argentinian cardinal if he had a copy, to which Bergoglio replied that he had spoken off the cuff. The Cuban cardinal pressed Bergoglio to sum up the essence of his intervention. The next day, Bergoglio gave Ortega a handwritten note. Ortega circulated the memorandum as an *aide memoire*, evidently hoping to influence his fellow cardinals.

In the text, Bergoglio had written,

> When the Church does not come out of herself to evangelize, she becomes self-referential and then gets sick. (cf. The deformed woman of the Gospel). The evils that, over time, happen in ecclesial institutions have their root in self-referentiality and a kind of theological narcissism. In the Book of the Apocalypse, Jesus says that he stands at the door and knocks. Obviously, the text refers to his knocking from the outside in order to enter but I think about the times in which Jesus knocks from within so that we will let him come out. The self-referential Church keeps Jesus Christ within herself and does not let him out.

These words impressed several cardinals.

Halfway through the meetings, news arrived that Cardinal Keith O'Brien, the Archbishop of Glasgow would not attend. In a statement he revealed that 'there have been times that my sexual conduct has fallen below the standards expected of me as a priest, archbishop and cardinal'. The cardinal's admission was prompted by the complaints of some priests who witnessed his conduct and had brought it to the attention of Archbishop Antonio Mennini, the papal nuncio to Britain, and eventually to the media.

Media commentators realised that no more than a dozen of the 115 cardinals entering the conclave were serious candidates. The vast majority were not considered *papabile*, material to be pope. Age and health were grounds on which most were considered to be excluded.

In order to present the selection, sometimes presented to the public as a contest, journalists settled on a few likely candidates. Few believed that the Austrian Cardinal Christoph Schönborn, the Archbishop of Vienna, would be elected. A third pope from middle Europe seemed unlikely. The dramatic exodus of Catholics from the Church in Austria in recent years seemed to preclude him. A member of the Dominican Order and a polyglot, he was nonetheless a competent theologian and administrator. He was also the editor of the *Catechism of the Catholic Church* and a man of wide cultural preparation.

The Canadian Cardinal Marc Ouellet, Prefect of the Congregation for Bishops seemed a likely choice if the new pope was to come from the New World. A former Archbishop of Montreal, the cardinal had worked for a decade in Colombia and was a competent linguist. Aged 68, he was considered an ideal age by many pundits.

Two other cardinals from North America were favoured by the media, in particular the Italian media. Cardinal Seán Patrick O'Malley of Boston had inherited a diocese in chaos following the resignation of Cardinal Bernard Law in 2002. Law had been implicated in the cover-up of clergy who had sexually abused children. O'Malley's simplicity as a Capuchin and his gentle manner made him an attractive candidate. Cardinal Timothy Dolan, the gregarious and expansive Archbishop of New York, proved popular with journalists who enjoyed his robust good humour.

South America presented a strong character in the person of Pedro Odilo Sherer, the Archbishop of Sao Paolo. A one-time curial official, he was respected for his engagement in the Brazilian Church. At 63 he promised to have a lengthy pontificate and would also be a pope from the largest Catholic country in the world.

If the papacy was to return to the Italians, media sources speculated on Cardinal Angelo Scola. Ordained for the Communion and Liberation Group founded by Don Luigi Giussani, the scholarly prelate was seen as Italy's best hope.

A theologian, he had already served as Patriarch of Venice.

Should the cardinals seek a young pontiff, and one from Asia, Tagle, the 55-year-old Archbishop of Manila seemed a good choice. The fact that he had been a cardinal for less than six months would weigh against him. Italians jested that they wanted a Holy Father, not an Eternal Father.

Most journalistic analysis was benignly intended. Reform of the Curia was a consistent theme, although what that reform would entail was unclear. Sorting out the Institute for Religious Works, persistently referred to erroneously as the Vatican Bank was also to be a task for the new pope. Declining Church attendance in Europe, as well as syncretic practices in South America were also challenges for the new pope. One observer, the Jesuit writer Rev. Thomas Reese summed it up by saying the cardinals wanted Jesus with a Masters in Business Administration.

THE ELECTION

Light rain was falling in St Peter's Square on Wednesday the 13th of March. Already a dense crowd had filled the piazza. It was just half an hour to go until 7.00 p.m. Would there be more black smoke as the second day of the conclave ended? Many people had gathered both the previous evening and that morning to witness black plumes of smoke rising from the chimney. Voices murmured quietly and many were praying.

Inside the Sistine Chapel, the new pope had passed the 77, or two-thirds, votes required to be elected. A warm applause ran though the ranks of the cardinal electors. They had completed their mission. The Church had a new pope.

Cardinal Bergoglio listened as the remaining votes were counted and called out by the Cardinal Scrutineer. Finally, when the tally had been made, the assistant Cardinal Dean, Giovanni Battista Re approached the Archbishop of Buenos Aires.

'Do you accept the canonical election?' he asked.

'I am a great sinner; trusting in God's mercy and patience, in suffering I accept,' came the reply.

'And what name do you take?'

'I will be called Francis.'

There was a momentary pause which turned into robust applause. The cardinals in a Chinese whisper passed the name, unusual yet familiar down the line. This was the first pope to take the name of Francis. Heads nodded, eyebrows rose. For some cardinals, it was a signal that he would make his unique mark. Others wondered what they had just done.

Monsignor Guido Marini, the Papal Master of Liturgical Ceremonies brought the newly-elected pope to the sacristy to the left of the High Altar. The small room is sometimes called the Room of Tears, as the impact of the cardinals' decision often causes the new pope to cry.

Changing from his scarlet robes into his white scimar, the pope declined to wear the red mozzetta, an elbow-length cape worn by the Roman pontiff. When offered a gold-jewelled pectoral cross, he reached out for the silver metal cross which he had worn since he became bishop in Argentina.

Several white boxes with red leather shoes in a number of sizes were laid out on a table. The tailor asked the pope what size shoe he wore. The pope looked at him. 'Why?' he asked. The tailor indicated the traditional red shoes, the shoes of the fisherman. 'These are fine with me,' Pope Francis said, looking down at his battered black shoes.

Outside in the square, the crowd waited for the Cardinal Proto Dean to announce the news of the election. The ballots were to be burned at 7.00 p.m.

Meanwhile, in the piazza the crowds waited as the iron hands on the clock of the towers of St Peter's moved towards the seventh hour. Rain fell softly. Strangers in the crowd offered shelter under their umbrellas. An intense quiet and calm had settled on the crowd.

Suddenly, at 7.06 p.m., smoke began to unfurl from the chimney atop the Sistine Chapel. Large screens had been erected so that the crowds could see.

'É bianco, il fumo è bianco' – 'it's white, the smoke is white!'

Excited voices rose in various languages throughout the square. All eyes were fixed on the tiny chimney. There was no doubt. Dense clouds of white smoke were billowing from the roof of the chapel. Cheers went up. *Viva il papa!* Nobody knew yet who the new pope was, but a pope had been elected and the people rejoiced in the fact that their Church once again had a leader.

Slowly, the great bells of St Peter's began to toll. Gathering pace, their sound was echoed as all the church bells rang throughout the city. People clapped and hugged, greeting each other in scores of languages. Like waves roaring towards the shore, shouts resounded across the expanse of the Square. *Viva il papa!*

Alerted to the news, thousands of Romans and visitors hastened to St Peter's. A new bishop had been chosen. As the rain suddenly stopped, all lowered their umbrellas and hoods. Finally the bells ceased, although white smoke continued to unfurl unabated through the chimney on the Sistine roof. The crowds moved as one body, surging towards the facade of the basilica. Within moments, the Swiss Guard marched from the barracks below the Apostolic Palace and marched up the steps of the basilica. A brass band played a sprightly march. Dispatches of the various Italian military corps, each complete with its brass band, followed immediately. The soldiers moved with mechanical precision, each in their loudly-coloured uniform.

Flags from every continent waved through the crowd, each wondering who the new pope would be. Occasionally shouts erupted – long live the pope! *Viva, viva!*

The bands continued to play merry marches as the crowds waited patiently. An hour had passed since the unfurling smoke had heralded the election. The rituals had to be observed. Firstly the pope received the congratulations and obedience of all the cardinals present, standing beside rather than sitting on the throne prepared in front of the High Altar.

With the cardinals, the new pope walked to the 16th-century Pauline Chapel, to pray before the Blessed

Sacrament. On either side of him were Michaelangelo's great last frescos, the martyrdom of St Peter and St Paul. The cardinals sang a *Te Deum* in gratitude for the new pope.

It was now time for Francis to present himself to the people of Rome, even though the Square was also thronged with foreigners. The windows in the upper corridor of the facade lit up. Soon the announcement would be made. Across the world, TV and radio networks broadcast the unfolding events.

Pope Francis paused and asked to telephone his predecessor who was watching the proceeding on television at Castel Gandolfo. Within moments he was put through to Benedict XVI. Once more, history would be made as the new pope and the pope emeritus greeted each other and offered good wishes and assurances of prayers for one another.

The red velvet curtains parted on the central balcony. Cardinal Jean Tauran emerged onto the loggia. Dazzled by the bright lights, he proclaimed the ancient words: '*Annuntio vobis gaudium magnum*' – 'I announce to you great news' – '*Habemus Papam*' – 'We have a Pope.'

The crowd roared once more with delight and flags unfurled in the hopes that the new pope might be from their homeland.

'*Eminentissimum ac Reverendissimum Dominum, Dominum Georgium Marium Sanctae Romanae Ecclesiae Cardinalem Bergoglio qui sibi nomen imposuit Francisum*' – 'The most eminent and most reverend Lord Cardinal of the Holy Rome, the Lord Jorge Mario Bergoglio, who has taken the name Francis.'

The crowd was silent for a moment before roars erupted again of *Viva il Papa*. With a name like Bergoglio was he Italian? But soon word spread. The pope is from Argentina, the first Latino pope! Shouts swooped up and down in the crowds. The South Americans began singing national songs. Those who had room jumped up and down with joy. For the Italians, it was enough that he had an Italian name. Here and there the plainchant tones of the Salve Regina floated from sallow skinned seminarians. The name Francesco rebounded throughout the square from thousands of voices.

Within moments, a red velvet and silk embroidered drape was hung from the balcony. A short while later, the red velvet curtains on the balcony parted once more. A large medieval crucifix, originally from Spain, was carried out ahead of the new pope. The crowd would soon see the new Roman pontiff. The cheers rose once again. 'Francesco, Francesco, Francesco!'

When he appeared on the balcony, the pope seemed overwhelmed by the sight of 150,000 cheering faces looking up at him. He raised his right hand in an uncertain salute. He stood uneasily to attention as the brass bands below played the Italian and Vatican anthems. The cardinals gathered on the adjacent balconies to see the reaction of the crowd to their new pope.

'*Buona sera!*' The greeting, warm and understated, drew delighted laughs from the crowd. That is not the way the pope should speak. For the Italians, he was one of them. 'You know, it's the duty of the cardinals to find a new pope. Well, it seems that they went almost to the end of the world to find him, but, here we are!'

Thanking everyone for the warm welcome, Francis directed his first thoughts to his predecessor, Benedict XVI. Inviting the people to pray simple prayers, the *Our Father, Hail Mary* and *Glory be,* he drew the crowd into one voice. Francis offered his blessing, but first asked the people to pray to God for him, in silence.

'Now I will bless you. But I'd like to ask you a favour, for your prayer to bless me as your bishop. Let's pray silently, your prayer for me.' He bowed his head. There was intense silence as the thousands in the square, and people of good will throughout the world prayed for the diminutive figure.

'I am going to bless you all and the entire world – all the men and women of good will ...' Placing a red stole on his shoulders, he traced the triple sign of the Cross as the new Bishop of Rome gave his blessing in Latin. The crowd continued to cheer and sing. 'I'm going to leave you now. Good night, and I wish you peace.'

By now sharp-eyed observers had noted that Francis had eschewed the traditional pontifical mantel. Instead of a jeweled gold cross he wore the simple metal cross used as bishop in Buenos Aires. Changes were in the air.

Turning to leave, the pope took the microphone again. Promising to make a visit the next day to a Marian church, he waved to the crowds. 'We will see each other soon. Good night and sleep well.'

Beside him stood Cardinal Agostino Villini, the Vicar of Rome, and Cardinal Cláudio Hummes, his Brazilian friend who had sat beside him during the conclave.

It was time for a well-deserved dinner. Guided to the black Mercedes, Francis chose to travel again in the minibus in which the cardinals returned to their residence. Seated in the middle of the cardinals, he chatted with them on the six-minute journey.

After supper, the new pope retired to his quarters. But sleep evidently eluded him. When the other cardinals had gone to their rooms, Francis emerged from his, dressed in black trousers and a black overcoat. He asked if there was a car available. An astonished driver fetched a car, and the pope asked if he could go for a drive. Little could the crowds which had wildly saluted him a couple of hours earlier know that their new spiritual father was watching them amused from the inside of a small Italian-made car.

The next morning, at 5.45 a.m., Francis emerged from his room. Again he was dressed in his black trousers, shoes and black pullover. The security detail which saw him wondered if he had forgotten he was pope.

A couple of hours later, having breakfasted with six cardinals who were also early risers, he was off to the Basilica of St Mary Major. Here he prayed before an icon of the Virgin Mary, *Salus Populi Romani* – the well-being of the Romans. The ancient image had been venerated for centuries in Rome's 5th-century basilica dedicated to the honour of Mary.

When the security officers tried to close the basilica to the public, Francis waved them away. 'Leave them alone. I am a pilgrim too.' As he left the church, he met the confessors, urging them always to be merciful to penitents who come to avail of the Sacrament of Penance and Reconciliation: 'Be kind. Be merciful, the souls of the faithful need your mercy.'

Leaving St Mary's he then went to collect his luggage at the clerical hostel on the Via del Clero beside Piazza Navona. Not suspecting he would be elected pope, he had left his belongings in his room.

Arriving at the Casa del Clero, the pope asked at the porter's desk for a bulb for the bedside lamp. He remembered it had blown. The surprised official gave the pope the bulb. A short while later the pope descended with his luggage, paid the bill, saluted everyone and returned to the Vatican. The bulb had been changed.

EARLY DAYS

Two days later, Pope Francis invited the media to a special audience in the Paul VI Hall. When he came out the front door of the *Domus Sanctae Marthae* where he had been staying, he was surprised to see a large car and escort. The Paul VI Hall is just 500 metres away. With his by now unmistakable arched eyebrows, he laughed and waved the car away. He then turned to his right and set off with his lumbering gait towards the hall.

The Vatican officials looked at each other in barely concealed exasperation. Shrugging helplessly, they set off after the leader of the world's 1.2 billion Catholics. This was not how they had imagined the pontificate would go. But they would need to get used to the changes on a daily basis.

In a break in his prepared text, the pope explained to the 5,000 media personnel which had covered the conclave his reason for selecting the name Francis. 'Let me tell you a story,' the pope began. Francis recounted how he sat listening to the votes echo around the Sistine Chapel. His name continued to reverberate. When the 77th ballot was called out, the cardinal realised that he had passed the required two-thirds majority. Applause broke out, but protocol demanded that the remaining votes be announced and tallied. During those moments, Cardinal Cláudio Hummes, the former Archbishop of Sao Paolo leaned over and embraced him.

Hummes whispered, 'Jorge, don't forget the poor!' Francis recalled the patron saint of Italy, the 13th-century figure who rejected the riches of his father's home in order to live with the sick and needy.

> The man of the poor. The man of peace. The man who loved and cared for creation – and in this moment we don't have such a great relationship with creation. The man who gives us this spirit of peace, the poor man. Ah – how I would like a Church which is poor and for the poor!

Francis of Assisi is the patron saint of Italy. The son of a prosperous fabric merchant in the Umbrian town of Assisi, Francis was born c.1181. Engaged as a soldier in a battle between the forces of Assisi and Perugia, Francis was wounded. Upon his recovery, Francis underwent a change of character. No longer a carefree youth, he now took an active interest in the poor and sick. Gathering a group of like-minded men around him, Francis encouraged them to look after the poor. They wore simple clothing, lived simply and went about preaching in simple language in the market places and streets of the towns.

Such was Francis' attraction that scores of followers enrolled in his band, which was finally supported by Pope Innocent III. His cheerful demeanour earned him the soubriquet 'God's troubadour'. Yet when he died he was found to have developed lesions on his side, hands and feet, similar to the markings of the crucified Jesus.

Francis died in 1226 and just two years later was canonised by Pope Gregory IX in one of the first acts of his pontificate. His order continued to flourish after his death. Although there were subsequent divisions, the Franciscans remain one of the most respected orders in the Church and Francis was proclaimed the patron saint of Italy. He remains one of the most admired religious figures to the present day.

Pope Francis revealed that some cardinals subsequently jested that he should have taken other names. 'How about Adrian IV, the great reformer.' This was a reference to the need to reform much of the Vatican bureaucracy. Another name they suggested was Clement XV, to get even with Clement XIV, who had suppressed the Society of Jesus, the Jesuits in 1773. Lest anyone be under the illusion that he might be serious, he added that these were good natured jokes.

As he took his leave of the media personnel, he offered his blessing. Speaking in Spanish he added:

> I told you I was cordially imparting my blessing. Since many of you are not members of the Catholic Church, and others are not believers, I cordially give this blessing silently, to each of you, respecting the conscience of each, but in the knowledge that each of you is a child of God. May God bless you!

On Sunday morning, the first of his pontificate, Francis chose to celebrate Mass in the parish church of St Anna. It was a marked contrast to his predecessors who chose to celebrate their first Sunday in their private chapel. Arriving at the church, which lies at the entrance to the Vatican, the pope went to greet the people who could not gain access to the crowded church. Speaking off the cuff during Mass, Francis spoke of the mercy of God. 'While we are prone to judge and not help, God's mercy can help us get over our weakness and help those in deeper need.'

At the end of the Mass, he introduced a number of priests who had come to concelebrate. He laughed as he said these were not members of the Vatican parish but rather had sneaked their way in. He took particular pleasure in introducing a priest from Argentina who worked with young people and tried to help them overcome problems with drugs.

He comes from far away. He is a priest who works with children and with drug addicts on the street. He opened a school for them; he has done many things to make Jesus known, and all those boys and girls off the street, they today work with the studies they have done; they have the ability to work, they believe and they love Jesus. I ask you Gonzalo, come, come and greet the people. Pray for him! He works in Uruguay, the founder of Jubilar Juan Pablo II. I do not know how he came here, but I will find out! Pray for him!

The congregation had never heard a pope speak like this and laughed as the pope gestured and waved to the priests.

Following the Mass, while still in his vestments, the pope went to the gates of the Vatican. To the horror of his security personnel, he lunged into the crowds, shaking hands and hugging some people whom he recognised. To the senior Vatican authorities, the greatest problem was the fact that he had crossed into Italian territory without any regard for protocol. Left unchecked, this would create a diplomatic and security nightmare.

That afternoon, there was a meeting between two popes. Given the influence Jesuits exercised in past centuries, the expression 'Black Pope' was applied to the General of the Order. As the first Jesuit pope, the General wrote to Francis, offering his congratulations and the good wishes of the conferees.

The pope was pleased to receive the letter and phoned the General House. The General, Fr Adolfo Nicolás, responded and the two had a cordial conversation. Pope Francis invited the General to visit him the next day at the *Domus Sanctae Marthae*. The General House is a five-minute walk from the Vatican. When the two met, the pope insisted that the General desist from addressing him as Holy Father or Your Holiness.

'I am a Jesuit!' bantered Francis.

The General offered him the resources of the Jesuit Order, knowing that Francis would be familiar with so many members and would appreciate counsel and competent personnel.

The General was undoubtedly aware of the tensions between Bergoglio and the central administration of the order. He knew that whenever Bergoglio visited Rome his first choice was to stay at the General House of the Dominican Order at Santa Sabina on the Aventine Hill. This was where Fr Carlos Azpiroz, the Master of the Dominican Order and fellow native of Buenos Aires lived and worked. Bergoglio did not stay at the Jesuit headquarters a few metres from the Vatican.

While the membership of Jesuits worldwide is close on nineteen thousand, the spread is uneven. As numbers decline in Europe and in the United States of America, vocations are increasing in Africa, Vietnam, and some South American countries. As the Jesuits have a vow of particular obedience to the pope, their collaboration cannot be underestimated.

The new pope was not an outsider to the Vatican. For many years he had been a member of several Vatican congregations, including the commission for Latin America although he rarely attended the annual plenary meetings in Rome. When asked why he left Rome after only a short visit on each occasion, he jested, 'I must get back to my wife, the diocese!'

In the early days of his pontificate, the pope was obliged to use the phone to contact friends. On the night of his election, he called his good friends, the journalists who had written his biography, *The Jesuit*. A few days later, the pope's former dentist received a call from the Vatican. The pope thanked him for his years of care, adding that he hoped they would meet again soon.

For some 20 years, Daniel Del Regno had delivered a newspaper to the bishop of Buenos Aires. When Pope Francis stepped out on the balcony on St Peter's on the night of his election, Del Regno realised that he had lost a customer. A phone call confirmed his fears. Although the voice claimed to be that of the new pope, the vendor was sure it was a friend playing a practical joke. 'No, truely, this is Jorge Bergoglio!' Speaking to the Argentine daily *La Nación*, Del Regno recounted the moment when he realised that it was indeed the pope, who proceeded to thank him for his years of faithful delivery and sent his good wishes to the Del Regno family.

In his first written message, Pope Francis addressed the Jewish community of Rome. The community is one of the oldest outside of the Holy Land. To mark the feast of Passover, the pope sent a letter to Rabbi Riccardo de Segni, thanking the rabbi of the Roman synagogue for his good wishes and expressing the hope of working together.

In Jorge Bergoglio's native country, people needed to be up early to watch the Mass to mark the beginning of the Petrine Ministry. Thousands crowded into the park in front of the Cathedral of Buenos Aires. The morning dew still clung to the grass and trees. Large screens were erected in the square so the crowds could see the broadcast from Rome. Several wrapped themselves in the blue and white national flag.

Shortly before the Mass began, a familiar voice came over the loudspeakers. A cheer went up as the crowd recognised the familiar voice. The pope was on the telephone.

'I want to ask you to walk together, and take care of one another.' said the voice. 'Do not cause harm. Protect life. Protect the family; protect nature; protect the young; protect the elderly. Let there not be hatred or fighting. Put aside envy. Don't take the hide of anybody,' The crowds laughed at the folksy expression, so familiar and true. 'Talk with one another so that this desire to protect each other might grow in your hearts. And draw near to God. God is good. He always forgives and understands. And don't forget that this bishop who is far away loves you very much. Pray for me.'

Spring had been an unseasonably cold and wet in Italy. Yet on 19 March, the day of the Mass to mark the beginning of the Petrine Ministry, the sun shone brilliantly. The bright flags of the crowds vied with the elaborate colours of the concelebrants. The pope chose to wear a simple, unadorned chasuble, with a brown strip from his homeland. It was a further tribute to St Francis, with whom the colour is traditionally linked.

Although the pope had asked the papal nuncio in Argentina to dissuade people and clergy from travelling from Argentina, there was a small delegation from the archdiocese. Among them was a young man, Sergio Sánchez. A cartonero, a poor man who makes money from collecting scrap paper, Sergio belonged to the Excluded Workers Alliance. He had met Archbishop Bergoglio on his visits to the slums of the city.

When he emerged from the basilica to the steps where Mass would be celebrated, the pope gave a warm welcome to his fellow Argentinian. Cardinal Angelo Sodano placed the pallium of office on his shoulders and the Ring of the Fisherman on his finger. With typical frugality, Francis had refused to commission a specially-made ring, but used a silver ring made for Pope Paul VI thirty-five years earlier by the artist Enrico Manfrini.

To honour the presence of Bartholomew I, the Patriarch of Constantinople, the Gospel was proclaimed in Greek rather than Latin. Meeting with ecumenical delegates the following morning, the pope thanked them all for coming. Bartholomew I met with the pope privately for 20 minutes. At the end of the meeting, the two agreed to travel to

Jerusalem together in 2014, to mark the fiftieth anniversary of the meeting of Pope Paul VI and Patriarch Athenagoras, when both men rescinded the mutual excommunications which led to the Great Schism between East and West in 1054.

That afternoon, the pope hosted friends and members of the Argentinian community in Rome. His two fellow natives of Buenos Aires, Cardinal Leonardo Sandri and Archbishop Marcelo Sánchez Sorondo joined a hundred well-wishers, men women and children during which the pope was presented with a jersey of his beloved San Lorenzo Football Club. The Pope quipped that he had not missed a single championship club match since 1946. 'There are not many fans who can say that,' the Pope laughed. 'Don't make me miss them now!'

The next morning, the pope celebrated Mass at 7.00 a.m. at the *Domus Sanctae Marthae*. The cardinals had all left and the pope remarked that the house seemed quite empty. The previous day, he requested Archbishop Georg Gaenswein to invite some people to the morning Mass. Thus the cooks and cleaners of the Domus were invited to the Mass in the main chapel.

This was the beginning of a new way of celebrating Mass. While Pope John Paul II regularly invited people to Mass in the Apostolic Palace, Pope Benedict XVI rarely invited guests. For Francis, the chapel was open to everybody. The following day, the street cleaners, garbage collectors and gardiners of the Vatican were invited. Later that morning, Luciano Cecchetti, one of the gardiners, expressed his disbelief at the invitation. 'Usually we're the invisible and forgotten ones.'

Each morning the pope continued the practice of inviting various workers in the Vatican, stopping to greet each one personally after Mass.

It was a sight never before seen in 2000 years of Christian history. While a handful of popes have abdicated, there is no record of any meeting between successor and predecessor. On Saturday 23 March, Francis left the Vatican by helicopter, bound for Castel Gandolfo to visit the pope emeritus in the country residence where Benedict XVI had stayed since 28 February.

Arriving at the landing pad at Castel Gandolfo, Pope Francis was surprised that Benedict had come to greet him personally. Emerging from the helicopter, Francis saw the elderly pontiff emeritus standing in the cold morning air. The retired pontiff wore a simple white soutane, with a white quilted Parka jacket to ward off the chill of the March day.

'Good morning! Thank you for your visit,' said Benedict as he welcomed his guest. He appeared more frail than when he made his last public appearance three weeks earlier. Francis smiled back. There was no protocol to govern the historic meeting. But this was a meeting between two old friends.

Turning to the car, the pair made the brief journey to the main villa. Entering the villa they were accompanied to the chapel. Benedict stood back to allow Francis enter the chapel. The latter was evidently slightly nervous. Benedict followed him, walking slowly with a cane, and indicated that he would kneel behind the pope. When Francis saw this, he turned towards the back of the chapel. 'No, no,' Benedict gestured towards the pontiff to kneel in the front. Francis took his hand. 'Please, let us pray together. We are brothers.' Benedict was evidently touched by the new pope's kindness, and both men knelt, side by side. No protocol could have foreseen the simplicity of the two pontiffs, joined together in prayer before the Tabernacle.

As a guest of the former pope, Francis brought a gift. With disarming simplicity, he admitted that the gift, an icon of the Madonna, had been chosen for him by his aides. 'It is the Madonna of Humility,' he explained. 'I did not know it before. If you don't mind me saying, but it reminds me of the many signs of humility you gave us in your pontificate.' The unexpectedly tender words caught Benedict by surprise, and he nodded. *'Grazie, grazie!'*

The two men then withdrew for a private dialogue of some three quarters of an hour, before lunching with the secretaries. Benedict personally renewed his obedience to the new pope. For Francis, it brought the dramatic period of forty days of Church events to a close. In the Christian calendar, Palm Sunday marks the beginning of the annual commemoration of the last week of Jesus' life. Recalling the entrance into Jerusalem, the people of Rome gather around the bishop to re-enact the jubilant day two thousand years earlier when Jesus received an ecstatic welcome to Jerusalem.

For Francis, this was another opportunity to meet with the immense crowds which packed St Peter's Square. In his homily, the pope announced that he would travel to Brazil in July to attend the World Youth Day. The young people gave him a rapturous applause. For the first time in twenty-five years the World Youth Day would be held in South America. The Latin American pope was coming home.

At the end of April 2013, the spokesman for the Holy See confirmed that the trip to Brazil would be his only overseas trip for 2013. He would not return to Argentina in the first year of his pontificate. However, he was expected to make a visit to Argentina some time in 2014. Before that, he was expected to make a visit to the tomb of St Francis of Assisi.

After the Mass, Pope Francis travelled through the crowds on the Popemobile. Several times he asked the driver to stop. He disembarked when he recognised some young people from Buenos Aires who vivaciously hugged and kissed him. When an elderly women reached out to touch him, he held her hand and kissed it.

Within days, the Vatican office organising the World Youth Day in Rio de Janeiro was overwhelmed with calls and emails concerning the July event. Bookings had to be revised upwards. Advance bookings indicated that as many as two million young people would attend the ceremonies which would be spread over the week 22–28 July.

Holy Week is the most sacred liturgical period in the Church's year, when Christians commemorate the death and resurrection of Jesus. The Jewish Passover or Pesach fell during the same days, and Francis sent his greetings to the Jewish community in Rome. It was the second time he had greeted Rabbi Di Segno in a week.

On the Monday of Holy Week, most of the forty priests who normally live in the *Domus Sanctae Marthae* returned to their rooms. They had vacated their home to make way for the cardinals during the conclave. The priests mostly serve in the Secretariat of State or other dicasteries. Although they knew the pope was still in residence, the priests were surprised to be invited to Mass the following morning in the residence chapel. Pope Francis said how much he enjoyed being in the Domus and sharing the fraternity with those who lived there. He indicated that he would not move into the Private Apartments in the Apostolic Place, where previous popes had lived. When he had visited them following his election, he had exclaimed that three hundred people could live in the space.

When Mass was over, the pope sat in the last bench at the back of the chapel. As the priests left, he stood and greeted each personally, thanking them for their service.

Taking his leave, he gave a large Easter egg which he had received as a gift to the clergy. The priests were bemused by the new tenant. In the coming weeks, Francis would become a familiar figure sitting at a round table with a glass of orange juice in his hand laughing and gesticulating with residents and visitors alike. The security detail observed the scene and tried to adapt. They hoped that he would soon settle into a routine.

The pope's first General Audience was attended by tens of thousands of enthusiastic pilgrims and tourists. Such numbers had not been seen since the pontificate of John Paul II. Francis pointedly spoke only in Italian, understood by some to underline his commitment to the Italian citizens of Rome. Such were the crowds that Francis toured the entire perimeter to salute the people. Before leaving, the pope saluted the disabled who were in attendance and even signed his name on the plaster of Paris cast of a young girl who had broken her leg.

On Holy Thursday, the pope presided over the Chrism Mass in St Peter's Basilica. Bishops and priests attended the annual Mass at which the Holy Oils used in the administration of the Sacraments were blessed. In his homily, the new pontiff gave the first hint of his expectations of priests. His message was demanding and critical of priests who do not fulfil their ministry. 'We need to go out to the outskirts where there is suffering, bloodshed, blindness that longs for sight, and prisoners in thrall to many evil masters.' By doing this, priests could be sure of the support of the people. Francis continued:

> Those who do not go out of themselves, instead of being mediators, gradually become intermediaries, managers. We know the difference: the intermediary, the manager, 'has already received his reward', and since he doesn't put his own skin and his own heart on the line, he never hears a warm, heartfelt word of thanks. This is precisely the

reason for the dissatisfaction of some, who end up sad – sad priests – in some sense becoming collectors of antiques or novelties, instead of being shepherds living with 'the smell of the sheep'.

For some who knew Bergoglio, these sharp words were familiar echoes of his high standards as a Jesuit superior and diocesan bishop.

Pope Francis' spontaneous nature appeared that morning. Meeting the Deputy Secretary of State, Archbishop Beccu, the pontiff asked him what he was doing for lunch. 'I am having some priests over to my apartment for a simple meal,' the archbishop said. It was a tradition he had kept up since he was Apostolic Nuncio in Angola and Cuba. 'May I come too?' came the unexpected request from the pope. The guests were mostly from the parishes of Rome, Don Angelo Donatis, Rector of the Parish of San Marco in Campidoglio, a well-known spiritual advisor to priests in the city. Monsignor Enrico Feroci, the director of Caritas, the social outreach programme of the diocese of Rome for the poor, was another guest. The other clergy worked with the poor and marginalised. The atmosphere at the table was relaxed. Pope Francis recalled several anecdotes of his life in Argentina. Before he left the priests, he advised them to pay particular attention to the Sacrament of Penance and Reconciliation. The idea occurred to him to write a letter to the homeless. When asked how it could be delivered, he said the priests could bring it personally. 'Put the light on the Confessional. You will see the people form a line when they see it,' he advised.

On Thursday afternoon, Francis broke a centuries-old tradition. Rather than celebrate the Mass of the Lord's Supper, the opening of the Easter Triduum, in the baroque splendour of St Peter's Basilica, the pope chose to visit the youth detention centre in a Roman suburb. During his years as bishop in Buenos Aires, Jorge Bergoglio celebrated

Mass with the poor. His choice as pope was the natural progression of his practice as bishop.

As he left the Vatican with Cardinal Agostino Vallini, vicar of the diocese of Rome, the roads were lined with well-wishers. The pope kept repeating the words 'incredible, incredible' as he looked out the window at the enthusiastic crowds.

According to the Principal, Liana Giambartolomei, the pope had asked that no other young people be present. He intended his visit to be solely for the 50 residents detained at the borstal. Of that number, only eight are Italian. While some were Catholic, others were Muslim or of no religion. A Caritas volunteer, who overheard one of the young detainees react to the unexpected news of the visit said 'At last I will get to meet somebody who claims he is my father!' For the first time in a papal liturgy, the pope washed the feet of Muslims and of a young girl. Before he left, the pope gave presents of Easter eggs and colomba, the traditional Easter cake.

Soon the pope settled into a routine. The guests at the house were bemused at their illustrious guest. Despite the security guards efforts, they regularly crossed paths with the pope. It was not unusual when the elevator doors opened to reveal the pope inside. Some of the residents were also irritated at the increased security which now surrounded the house and occasionally made access difficult.

Francis took it all in his stride. Seeing a Swiss Guard standing outside his room one evening, the pope suggested that he be seated. The young guard replied that he was obliged to guard the pope during the night and had to remain standing. The pope went into his room and brought out a chair. 'I am going to bed,' he said. 'I can give you an order to sit down.' The young guard was perplexed but finally obeyed. Some moments later, the pope returned with a snack. 'Standing there, you must be hungry,' he said, before wishing the guard a good night.

Francis settled into a routine at the *Domus Sanctae Marthae*. Each morning, he celebrated Mass at 7.00 a.m., and continued to invite people who worked in the Vatican City State, preaching off the cuff on the Scriptural readings. Observers noted both his style and the content. Such was the interest in these informal homilies that Vatican television began to broadcast them on the Vatican news website. The brief meditations were suitable for soundbites.

Speaking towards the end of April at Mass attended by some members of the Institute for Religious Works, Francis hinted that there would be changes. Bureaucracy is a hinderance if it gets in the way of love, he noted. At the General Audiences he bantered between the crowds, especially in his exchange with young people. He regularly broke off from his prepared text to recount an anecdote or to offer a brief reflection. Often these were provocative. Citing the Gospel where Jesus urges a welcome for the stranger, the pope paused. 'That is true. Welcome the stranger. How many foreigners there are in this diocese of Rome. Yes, and what do we do for them?' He shrugged his shoulders.

The enormous numbers which attended the public ceremonies and audiences showed no sign of abating. Although he had learned German, French and English, he felt uncomfortable speaking them. He often excused his accent, explaining that English gave him most difficulty. But his homely, if not always quite accurate, Italian charmed everybody.

Vatican officials were getting used to Pope Francis' eccentricities. Noticing that all the lights were on in the

Apostolic Library one sunny morning, he asked an assistant to turn them off. 'That will keep the bills down,' he commented wryly.

At the *Domus Sanctae Martae*, the pope also insisted on turning lights off in the corridors when there was nobody around. One exasperated curial official complained to a colleague 'The Latin American bishops are always difficult to deal with. And a Latino Pope is impossible.'

The natural cycle for the beginning of the pontificate came to an end as the pontiff took possession of the cathedral of Rome, St John Lateran. Built in the early 4th century by the emperor Constantine, the Lateran Basilica and palace had served as the bishop's cathedral and residence for a millennium. Even when the popes moved to live in the Vatican in the 19th century, they retained the Lateran as their official seat.

As he entered the basilica, the pope was almost mobbed by the crowds which had gathered. With a broad smile, Pope Francis lunged into the outstretched arms. As he had repeatedly said since his election, he was bishop of Rome and thus had to be with the people.

During the Mass, the pope carried the aluminum pastoral staff made by the Neapolitan sculptor Lillo Scorzelli for Pope Paul VI in 1965. Benedict XVI ceased using the austere cross when he received a gift of a more traditional ferule cross in 2009 from the Circle of St Peter, a charitable confraternity founded in 1869. The return to the simple crucifix, which had also been used by John Paul I and John Paul II, seemed to be a further rupture from the liturgy as had been celebrated by Pope Benedict.

He reiterated the message the following Sunday when he ordained ten men in St Peter's Basilica, exhorting the new priests to be 'pastors, not functionaries. Be mediators, not intermediaries.'

The pope announced that he would begin a series of Sunday visits to the 335 parishes of Rome, following his meeting with ecclesial groups at Pentecost in May. The first parish, of Santi Elisabetta e Zaccaria, was on the periphery of Rome. As was his custom in Buenos Aires, the pontiff would give children of the parish their First Communion.

By now, the lines of the new pontificate were clear. Although no longer administering an Argentinian diocese of 2.5 million, Francis continued in the style and conviction developed over a lifetime. Just two days prior to his election, he had quietly observed 55 years since he began his training with the Jesuits and on 22 April he marked the 40th anniversary of his final profession.

Cardinal Bergoglio had been contemplating his immanent retirement when he heard of Benedict XVI's resignation. Now he had responsibility for the world's 1.2 billion Catholics as well as to other Christians and members of the world's faiths.

Within two weeks of his election, Francis appointed his former auxiliary bishop, Mario Aurelio Poli as his successor. He likewise nominated the Spaniard, José Rodriguez Carballo, Master General of the Franciscan Friars Minor as the Secretary of the Congregation for the Institute of Religious.

While he could not compete with the high theology of his predecessor, the 'Professor Pope,' Francis' simple and brief homilies and speeches were profound and touching. Although Francis consistently referred to himself as Bishop of Rome, the role was not simply confined to the diocese. Since the first century the administration at Rome intervened in the affairs of other dioceses. That waxed and waned during subsequent centuries. However, in the 20th century, papal power reached its apogee under John Paul II whose global journeys brought him some 698,310 miles

(1,123,322 km), 28 times around the earth or 3 times the distance between the earth and moon. Karol Wojtyla's energy was legendary. He was 58 when he was elected to the papacy; Jorge Bergoglio was already 76.

Soon the routine of receiving Heads of State and addressing delegations would be added to the increasing workload. The Italian bishops were among the first to be received as they made their *ad limina* visit to the pope and the Holy See. The visits made by the world's some five thousand bishops were served as an important link between Rome and local bishops. While the bishops in general are successors of the apostles, only the Bishop of Rome can lay claim to being the successor of St Peter.

A month after his election, it was time for the new pope to turn his attention to pressing matters. If his pontificate was to be more than gestures, he needed to provide firm governance. On his retirement, Pope Benedict had left Francis a number of documents which included a 300-page report prepared by Cardinals Julián Herranz, Salvatore De Giorgi and Josef Tomko. This was the summary of their investigation into the leaked documents discovered in the Spring of 2012. Another document concerned the governance of the universal church. Having read the reports, Francis addressed the issues quickly and decisively.

There were two overlapping issues which needed to be dealt with. The first concerned the manner in which the pope governed the Church while the second called for a streamlining of the Roman curia. The last time a reform of the curia had been undertaken was by Pope Paul VI in his Apostolic Constitution, *Regimini Ecclesiae Universae*, published in 1967. Establishing a committee of eight cardinals from five continents to assist him, Pope Francis' advisory board included Francisco Javier Errázuriz Ossa of Santiago, Chile, Oswald Gracias of Bombay, Reinhard Marx of Munich, Laurent Monsengwo Pasinya of Kinshasa, Sean

Patrick O'Malley of Boston, George Pell of Sydney and Giuseppe Bertello, governor of Vatican City State. Óscar Andrés Rodríguez Maradiaga of Tegucigalpa, Honduras was appointed to co-ordinate the group.

Historians noted that this form of consultation had not been seen in over a millennium, when the five patriarchs of Rome, Constantinople, Alexandria, Jerusalem and Antioch were in regular correspondence. Although not due to meet until October, the pontiff began to consult regularly with them by telephone and mail. Former colleagues recalled that although Bergoglio consulted widely, he always took decisions alone. His Jesuit training of discernment came to the fore, as he considered the various situations presented to him from all angles.

Many hoped that with a Latin pope, outmoded forms of ecclesiastical offices and exaggerated forms of address and offices would be abolished. The contribution of women in the Church needs to be fostered and acknowledged with more than mere lip service. The historical nature of the Church's development explains some of the myopic misogynism. But this attitude must come to an end and Francis seems to promise much in this regard.

His swift and firm resolution of banking scandals inherited as Archbishop of Buenos Aires also presaged well for restructuring of the Vatican's financial system which had long been exploited by dishonest clients. Cardinal Óscar Andrés Rodríguez Maradiaga hinted that the pope intended to unite the various economic administrations under one single office. Such a move would end centuries of dispersion, where various parts of the Vatican or Holy See were administered separately. Although unification had been one of Pope Paul VI's intentions he never achieved it during his pontificate.

Competent lay men and women could move to a central part in the administration of the offices of the Holy See.

Such changes would help end the damaging careerism which saw clergy spend their whole working lives in offices which were only intended for a five-year term. Jesuits take a promise to avoid high ecclesiastical office. For Jorge Bergoglio, such careerism was not acceptable.

The global face of Catholicism continued to develop and change. There was the problem of persecuted Catholics and Christians in various countries, the underground Church in China, the scandal of clerical paedophilia, waning ecumenism, and loss of faith in former Christian countries. In addition, Francis' attention would be needed for the thousands of Latino Catholics in both South and North America who abandoned their native faith in favour of the evangelical sects. When meeting with Latin American bishops for their annual visit at the end of April, he urged them not to produce more documents but a plan to engage with people.

This was the Year of Faith, which Benedict XVI had called in 2012 to mark the 50th anniversary of the Second Vatican Council. For Francis, these months provided an opportunity to encourage the people to remain firm and deepen their Catholic faith.

It was inevitable that Francis' election would not be met with universal approval; having enjoyed such a promising start, Francis was bound to disappoint some people. In his own country calls from the mothers and grandmothers of the victims of the Dirty Wars called on his intervention. But even a pope could not unravel the horrific threads of murder and torture carried out by the military juntas.

The Pope pushed forward the beatification of Archbishop Oscar Romero of El Salvador, the outspoken and tenacious proponent of human rights, who had been assassinated while celebrating Mass on 24 March 1980. The Pope's intervention unblocked the cause which had stalled for several years. It was one more signal of the direction the pontificate was taking.

By now three of Francis' siblings had died, leaving him with one remaining sister but he remained close to his family. Most recently, his brother Alberto Horacio had died in May 2010. His late sister Marta, who had died in 2007, had two sons and a daughter with her husband Enrico Narvaja, Pablo, a teacher, José Luis, who like his uncle had become a Jesuit and María Inés. María Elena had two sons, Juan and Jorge. She invited her brother to become Jorge's godfather. But he was far from his 'spouse' Buenos Aires, and far from his people. He could no longer experience the smells, the noises and the hustle and bustle of his native land. Despite his fondness for the telephone, it would never be a substitute for those face-to-face encounters on which he had thrived. Now an elderly man, an enormous task awaited him engaging the hopes and expectations of millions.

The eloquent proponent of Liberation Theology, Leonardo Boff, pithily summed up the extraordinary events which led the first Latino pope to the Throne of Peter:

> Bergoglio's past does not matter.
> What matters is Francis' future.